Twayne's United States Authors Series

EDITOR OF THIS VOLUME

Warren French

Indiana University

Gerald Warner Brace

TUSAS 384

Gerald Warner Brace

GERALD WARNER BRACE

By Joseph Lovering

Canisius College

TWAYNE PUBLISHERS
A DIVISION OF G. K. HALL & CO., BOSTON

Copyright © 1981 by G. K. Hall & Co.

Published in 1981 by Twayne Publishers,
A Division of G. K. Hall & Co.
All Rights Reserved

Printed on permanent/durable acid-free paper and bound
in the United States of America

First Printing

Library of Congress Cataloging in Publication Data

Lovering, Joseph P   1921–
Gerald Warner Brace.

(Twayne's United States authors series ; TUSAS 384)
Bibliography: p. 183–84
Includes index.
1.   Brace, Gerald Warner, 1901– —Criticism and interpretation.
PS3503.R14Z75   813'.52   80–29071
ISBN 0-8057-7318-5

For Eileen
Whose help is all ways

Contents

"Jerry"

I first heard of Gerald Warner Brace just before leaving Chicago for Boston in the fall of 1947, when a clerk in a Michigan Avenue book shop called my attention to *The Garretson Chronicle* as one of the finest new novels. When I arrived at Boston University, I learned not only that he was to be one of my colleagues but that, having read and liked my *Cavalcade of the English Novel,* he was eagerly awaiting my arrival.

From then until my retirement and his, followed by the shock of his death, our friendship never faltered. Even when we did not see eye to eye, I could always count on his loyalty and understanding. I wrote about him (and used him as a critic) when I was working on *Cavalcade of the American Novel,* and I dedicated my book on Emerson to him. I also reviewed everything that he published from this time forward, at first in the *Chicago Tribune Magazine of Books* and later in other media.

I still think I like the *Chronicle* best, though my weakness for fantasy and parable brings *A Summer's Tale* very close to me. This book is wholly characteristic of Brace only in its passion for islands. It suggests Byron, Melville, Peacock, Gilbert and Sullivan, and Aldous Huxley, yet it is not really derivative of any of them. Brace himself, I think, tended to prefer *Light on a Mountain,* and it is certainly true that *The Spire* is a better integrated book than the *Chronicle.*

If his central theme is the young New Englander growing, sometimes painfully, into life, his greatest gift was his capacity to catch the "feel" of New England and put it on paper. He knew how to tell a story, and he could write dialogue in which his people talk themselves alive. He could be wry and wise, shrewd and bitter, profoundly ironical and incorrigibly idealistic, all at the same time. In *The Spire,* for example, both the mossbacks and the sophisticates are handled satirically, without the author's rooting for either side. There are "dark" places in both *The Spire* and the *Mountain,* but if *Bell's Landing* is his darkest book, even here the darkness does not win.

"Jerry" by Edward Wagenknecht

I was surprised when he stopped writing fiction with *The Department;* when I asked him about it, he said he could not think of any more stories to tell. He obviously felt that the novel had fallen upon evil days, as indeed it has, but this seemed to me only to increase our need for the kind he could write. I think he was more concerned about being in touch with the *Zeitgeist* than was I, who could never see why it was more important to achieve harmony with the period in which one's lot had chanced to be cast than any other, the vital thing being merely the writer's own temperament and sense of values, and this may well be the reason why he became a novelist while I, for the most part, have confined myself to non-fiction. But there was never any question about Brace's fidelity to his own values, and I am happy to remember him among those whose books and whose friendship have enriched my life.

EDWARD WAGENKNECHT

Preface

The novels of Gerald W. Brace first attracted my attention in 1946 when I was a returning G.I. at Boston University Graduate School in English, where Mr. Brace was instructing. His courses always drew well because there was a sense of the genuine in them. As a professional writer he had an absorbing interest in both the stories and in the men and women who wrote them. Equally there was a genuineness about the teacher's concern for the neophyte scholars under him. Perhaps it mattered, too, that this was my first contact with an artist. I did not get to know Mr. Brace personally at that time; nor have I had the opportunity, aside from two visits with him after his retirement, to know him other than through his books. But over the years as my reading in his novels continued, my admiration for this writer grew.

It is clear that critics have made an implicit judgment at least about the value of Brace's novels by the fact that there have been no scholarly articles or books on his fiction. However, at the same time it is very clear from the many favorable reviews (especially as the quality of the writing continued consistently to be of a very high merit) that he commanded the respect of the critics. It is my judgment that his novels deserve attention and that their actual strengths lie in those qualities of writing which are not so esteemed by modern readers.

I have aimed to acquaint my readers with the eleven novels of Brace by giving fairly full summaries of each story. My focus is upon the New England that was the setting for all of his fiction. I have found these books to be noteworthy for their pervasive honesty about twentieth-century existence in New England. In one sense they may be taken as chronicles of the lives of ordinary Yankees of the early decades of the twentieth century. They reveal Gerald W. Brace as a creative writer of moral integrity and with a vision of man which has its roots in classical humanism. Mr. Brace's humanism is well tempered. He is for me something like Saul Bellow's Mr. Sammler. People around him might conceive of him as rather isolated. But that would only appear to be the case. He was intensely aware of all that went on about him and just as intensely interested in it. The ability to reflect on man's nature and destiny marked Brace's outlook; this is what makes reading him still worthwhile.

I hope I have in some measure occasioned readers to look again, or, for the first time, at these novels.

JOSEPH P. LOVERING

Canisius College
Buffalo, New York

Acknowledgments

I am indebted to several colleagues at Canisius College for their encouragement and for their responses to some of the novels of Gerald W. Brace.

I wish to thank the staff members of the Mugar Library at Boston University for their help with the special collection of Brace materials housed there; the Conant Library at Harvard University; and all the staff of Andrew L. Bouwhiss Library at Canisius College.

I wish to thank George Brockway, Chairman of the Board of W. W. Horton Co., both for the loan of the Brace files and for his offer to read my manuscript.

Mrs. Gerald W. Brace extended her hospitality to me graciously on several occasions. I further wish to thank her for her kind permission to quote from the works of her late husband.

My thanks go as well to Mrs. Ana Reinhold for the difficult task of typing my first draft; to Mrs. Adelaide Schroeder for her help on interlibrary loans. My daughter, Mary Edholm, deserves my gratitude for the excellent typing of my final draft. Professor Richard J. Thompson was most helpful in reading my manuscript and in making suggestions for improvement. Finally, I wish to express my thanks to Canisius College for the times I was freed to work on my project.

Chronology

1901   Gerald Warner Brace born at Islip, New York, on September 23, the fifth child of Charles Loring Brace and Louise (Warner) Brace.

1918   Graduates from Loomis School at Windsor, Connecticut.

1922   Graduates from Amherst College, where influential teachers were Professor George F. Whicher and Robert Frost; travels in Europe.

1922–   Attends Harvard Architectural School.
1923

1924   M.A. in English from Harvard.

1924–   Teaches at Williams.
1926

1927   Marries Huldah Laird on December 3.

1928–   Instructor and Tutor at Radcliffe.
1930

1930   Part-time instructor and tutor at Harvard; Ph.D. in English; thesis: "A Study of Literature in Relation to the Fine Arts in England 1650–1750." Travels in Europe.

1930–   Instructor at Dartmouth. Charles Loring Brace IV born
1934   in Hanover, December 1930.

1932   Gerald Warner Brace, Jr., born in Hanover, February 26.

1934–   Teaches at Mount Holyoke College.
1939

1934   Barbara Brace (Mrs. Ralph Seeley) born in Hanover, March 28.

1936   *The Islands*, Brace's first novel, is published by G. P. Putnam's. A single course at Amherst.

1938   *The Wayward Pilgrims*, novel.

1940   Begins long teaching career at Boston University.

1941   *Light on a Mountain*, novel. Belmont, Massachusetts, becomes permanent residence.

1947   *The Garretson Chronicle*, novel, becomes a best seller.

1949   *A Summer's Tale*, novel.

1952   *The Spire,* novel.
1955   Visiting Professor at Harvard. *Bell's Landing,* novel.
1955   Mediterranean cruise; Summer teaching at Harvard; guest lecturer at New Hampshire Writer's Conference.
1956   Appointed University Lecturer for 1956–57 at Boston University; "The Age of the Novel": University Lecture. Writer's Conference.
1957   *The World of Carrick's Cove,* novel.
1960   *Winter Solstice,* novel.
1964   *The Wind's Will,* novel.
1966   *Between Wind and Water,* novel; honorary degree— Doctor of Letters—from Southwestern Massachusetts Tech.
1967   Shell Distinguished Writing Award at Boston University; retirement from Boston University; teaches part time for two years.
1968   *The Department,* novel.
1969   *The Stuff of Fiction,* essays on the craft of fiction.
1970   Litt. D., Amherst.
1976   *Days That Were,* autobiography.
1978   Dies, July 20, in Blue Hill, Maine, of cancer.

CHAPTER 1

A Full Measure

WHEN he was seventy-six years old, Gerald W. Brace wrote a book called *Days That Were*, an autobiographical memoir of his early life through his twenty-first year that is of primary interest and value for anyone who desires to know the background of the writer. Like the autobiography of Anthony Trollope, the English novelist whom Brace came to appreciate and admire very much, *Days That Were* is remarkable for both its utter honesty about the crosscurrents of Brace's life and the revelation of the warmth of friendships made, many of which were sustained over a lifetime. Viewed through an objective recounting of events, Brace's life appears to have been a very ordinary one, especially when compared to the usual flamboyant accounts of writers' lives printed on dust jackets or written up as biographical sketches. Viewed from the inside, however, Brace's personal history provides not only an illumination of the man behind the books but a revealing glimpse into the mores of a significant segment of American society. I rely, therefore, largely on *Days That Were* to acquaint the reader with this writer.

Great-grandfather John Pierce Brace (1795–1872) was editor of the *Hartford Courant* and a teacher of Harriet Beecher Stowe of Litchfield, Connecticut. He is captured significantly in Stowe's *Old Town Folks*, a novel Gerald Brace holds important for its drawing of New England characters. J. P. Brace was himself a novelist with three published stories, two of which are adventures in the mode of Cooper. As Mr. Rossiter in *Old Town Folks*, Brace's grandfather is given a full-length portrait, especially through a letter that Rossiter writes to his sister: "And I am in my nature a Puritan as thoroughly as a hound is a hound, and a pointer, whose pedigree of unmixed blood can be traced for generations back. I feel within the preaching instinct, just as the hound sniffs, and the pointer points; but as to the pulpit in these days,—well thereby hangs a tale."[1] Brace sees his great grandfather as a warm human being of many fine accomplishments discouraged (like Hawthorne) by the Civil War.

His son, Charles Loring Brace, was born in 1826. He founded and headed the New York Children's Aid Society, an organization which was vital in the care and supervision of the poor and whose efforts to give the underprivileged youngsters a new environment in rural areas set the pace for other such organizations into our own times. He became friends with some of the great figures of the Victorian period, including John Stuart Mill, Sir Charles Lyell, Asa Gray, and James Bryce. C. L. Brace II, the novelist's father, was, too, a scholarly man, who grew up in Hartford, a friend of the influential American religious thinker, Horace Bushnell. Gerald Brace reflects upon his father as a faithful Christian but one who would have declared himself an agnostic if the matter were pressed upon him. He established a residence called "Ches-Knoll" in Dobbs-Ferry, New York, which became the home of Gerald W. Brace during his earliest years.

Brace describes his mother in these words: "My mother believed in God and heaven, and made us go to the Episcopal Church, and my father, Charles Loring Brace II, stayed home— he said he was a Unitarian and didn't have to go to church. He always made a joke of it, and whether he was really a Unitarian or not I never knew" (p. 36).[2] As his mother grew older she became saddened by the moral condition of the modern world. She didn't talk about it and, adds Brace, "I know she was troubled by some of the minor moral irregularities in the novels I began to write many years later, and she would be overwhelmed by the moral and religious anarchy of the present world" (p. 38).

Gerald Brace was the youngest of five children—there were two older sisters, Dorothy and Eleanor, and an older brother, Charles who became a hero and model. Their home was large and situated on the periphery of Dobbs Ferry, near a mansion of the Rockefellers, though the Braces were not in that financial category. The boys made friends with the lower-class Irish Catholics. Their exploits together and their friendships became the basis for one part of Brace's best known book, *The Garretson Chronicle*. Life at Ches-Knoll was relatively tranquil. Brace speaks of his family as mainly "cautious and somewhat repressed Yankees who keep their emotions and desires under control . . .," except for the Scots-Irish Neills and particularly cousin

Lamour Neill, a rambler and a ladies' man who added a dash of
color to a placid life style.

During the Ches-Knoll period Brace went for summer
vacations to the Maine Coast, beginning with a rented house at
North Haven when he was two; then at Mill Island (near Deer
Isle) which was the true beginning of his romance with the Maine
Coast. The family came in full entourage (four children, cook and
maid, family pets and trunks) from Dobbs Ferry to New York by
train; hence to Fall River by boat; next by train to the South
Station in Boston where the family rented a hotel room for the
day, letting the children paddle in the swan boats in the Public
Gardens; then an overnight sail on the "Bangor Boat" to
Rockland or to Deer Isle or thereabouts. The era of the summer
visitors to Maine was getting into full swing early in the new
century. Large houses called "cottages" were being built in the
nineties and the Braces occupied such a one on Mill Island until
1912. The jacket illustration of *Days That Were* superbly done
by the author shows the large shingled "cottage" mounted on
rock and set in fir trees with a southward view to the sea (pp.
60–72).

For Gerald W. Brace this coastal region was from the
beginning a source of true delight. He came eventually to
translate much of that deep feeling he had for his land and its
people into his stories: "It may seem that I am looking back too
sentimentally, but I know that for us young ones the early Deer
Isle summers were as purely happy as life could possibly be.
There was no sorrow for us, no loss, no failure of hope, no
concern about anything—except the passing of the lovely days"
(p. 77).

Brace's boyhood also was filled with the adventure of camping
with his father who loved to canoe and fish in the inland regions
of Maine. Apparently the son became an apt student. Later, on
fishing expeditions in eastern Maine at Grand Lake Stream, he
heard a Scotsman, Dugal, sing the ancient ballads of his home
land. Brace was then fifteen and later vividly recalled "a wholly
authentic folk tradition, untouched by anything literary or
scholastic, and it was for me a unique experience."

When he was nine the family moved from Dobbs-Ferry to New
York City, where his father continued to be involved with the
social-aid institutions which the grandfather had established.
There he was sent to a boys' private school on 56th St. Two years

later he attended the Gunnery School in Washington, Connecticut. Memories of this school evoke in the novelist's memory Dickensian images, e.g., of "Pa," the eighth-grade tyrant, yanking two youngsters before the group "like a Cruikshank illustration for *Nicholas Nickleby.*" The school wasn't too strong academically. It stressed its graded football elevens. Brace had his start with Latin at the Gunnery School and got along well enough with Caesar, but not Virgil. Sherlock Holmes and Zane Grey were the real food for his imagination. He smuggled them into the study area as textbooks. Next came the Loomis School in Windsor, Connecticut.

Loomis had been founded as a school which trained its students in practical matters such as business and farming. Brace ran the school's weekly newspaper and fancied himself becoming renowned as a marathon runner. The war was on in Europe, but Brace and his classmates had a vague Christian hope or vision of an orderly universe that would somehow prevail. It was based, he felt, on "the sentimental romantic Protestantism of the Victorian era which held that pious virtue was the safest road to success." His boyish conscience seemed to trouble him a little because of the good summer times in Maine when others were helping the cause. Brace affirms in many places that he was not by nature a joiner or even a good committeeman and that even if he were old enough to sign up, the army perhaps did not lose such a great prospect. His lifelong tendency of going his own way he himself attributes to a kind of social fear. Brace looking back, seems to have had some reservations about the elitism and group privilege that exclusive prep schools engender. But he hesitates to censure them for seeking out talented youngsters and offering them intellectual opportunities.

Brace's family were Yale oriented but his associations at Loomis brought him into contact with Amherst, which proved to be a fortunate collegiate experience. The college did not provide lodgings for its students. It fell to the students to find places for themselves in the town. Brace thus met Mrs. Carrie Johnson: "She assumed that I was a wayward son in need of maternal management, and I accepted her with irresistable delight." She was an eager, loving person with an intense interest in all the affairs of the young men who came to live with her. Brace in *The Garretson Chronicle* painted her as the warm, maternal Mrs. Seth Kingsley, whom Ralph meets on her farm on the outskirts of the town and who enters his life, with her whole family, and remains a steadfast friend. Brace continued to visit the Johnsons even when he no longer boarded there. He taught them how to drive their new Model T Ford. He felt as though he had been adopted by them. Mr. Johnson was a quiet and indulgent husband and Brace admired both husband and wife for their New England ways. Carrie Johnson's friendship remained a large inspiration in Brace's later life, but there was an unhappy ending to the story of the friendship with the Johnsons. When Carrie Johnson died, another woman quite her opposite took over house and husband. The matter ended with the suicide of Arthur Johnson, who was unable to live with the changed situation. Suicides in Brace's novels are not an infrequent occurrence; they may well have their beginning in the tragic end of Arthur Johnson.

Brace's great love of New England, its towns and its peoples, began at Amherst through his love for the Johnsons. He passed up academic awards in favor of long tramps through the countryside to villages such as New Salem, Conway, or Shelbourne, paying a dollar to stay overnight at a farmhouse and fifty cents for a dinner. He went long distances into Vermont. On his first foray into southern Vermont, Brace came at the end of a thirty-five-mile hike to the home of the Hancocks near Jacksonville. Like the Johnsons the Hancocks became his fast friends. They represented much of the New England that he began to search for.

Following the pattern of many artists before him, Gerald Brace did not cover himself with academic glory. But he did find those things that he needed to develop to become a writer. In his sophomore year he encountered Robert Frost who was just then beginning his long career as artist in residence in American colleges. Brace was as puzzled as the next person about the meaning of Frost's verses but the manner of the man in his informal talkative approach in class was unforgettable: "He said with his usual touch of irony that 'all there is to writing is having ideas,' and if any man was ever gifted with ideas it was Robert Frost: they flowed from him in a life-long stream, which as he said of West-running Brook is 'time, strength, tone, light, life and love.' The smallest details of his daily living were translated into emblems of universal experience . . ." (pp. 210–211). Brace is modest about his friendship with Robert Frost and certainly does not overstate their relationship in his autobiographical *Days That Were*. However, he did keep in contact with Frost over the years beyond Amherst. Frost helped him to get a teaching position at Amherst, and Brace entertained him on one occasion and introduced him to a Boston University audience. Reflections of Frostian tones and points of view can be found many times in Brace's work.

Brace calls George F. Whicher his master. Whicher's thorough knowledge of the New England Puritan background, his fine reading of poetry in class, his informal methods in "creative writing" and even his habit of "brisk" country walks caught Brace's fancy: "It was his example and encouragement that eventually turned me into the way of a student and teacher of English and a writer" (p. 213).

Brace recalls that Alexander Meiklejohn, the new president of Amherst, had the full respect of himself and other students who were appreciative of his efforts to make Amherst a place for real learning. If he had been aware of Frost's antagonisms and quarrels with Meiklejohn (as related in Thompson's biography of Frost), Brace admits that "it would have shocked me."

Sex was surrounded with mystery—there was nothing taught about it, and though there was some talk about it, the majority of boys lived in innocent idealism. *Days That Were* is as delightfully candid about sexual matters as it is on every other phase of growing up:

It is hardly necessary to say that sexual indulgence has always persisted in human affairs, but back in 1920 the restraints were dominant among most of us. We were aware of sin, and had no uncertainties about what it was. . . . Certainly I was magnetized and excited by girls, but until I met the girl I married I never even kissed one. It was not a question of moral principle, but of the manners and social customs we had been brought up with—though perhaps some sort of theory of moral behavior did make an unseen underpinning to our practice. We took such values for granted. But of course I was a good deal of a prig, which means I was devoted to the idea of virtue without any understanding of the true human forces I was involved in. (p. 218)

Graduation from Amherst was capped by a trip to Europe. Brace was particularly taken by a viewing of the cathedral of Amiens, which he calls "one of the major dramatic moments" of his life: "For a young romantic still imbued with the miraculous possibilities in human achievement it was an experience of genuine religious revelation. I thought it transcended all rational explanations; if God could inspire men to do such work there could seem to be no doubt as to His place in the scheme of the cosmos" (p. 238). Later he met his older sister Eleanor for a walking tour through the Alps, where he remembered Hilaire Belloc's *The Path to Rome,* a text that Professor Whicher had effectively introduced into his writing seminar.

Brace studied architecture for one year at Harvard in 1923 before switching to the study of literature. He took the M.A. degree in English in 1924. On several occasions Brace has paid sincere tribute to Russel Lebaron Briggs, then Dean at Harvard. On one occasion he said that Briggs was particularly helpful to Frost when the poet felt surfeited with Latin and Greek and wished to leave Harvard. Frost never forgot the sympathetic hearing he received. Possibly Brace received a similar treatment at the hands of Briggs.

When Gerald Brace married Huldah Laird in December 1927, he was launching his teaching career, which was to include, besides his part-time assistantship at Harvard, appointments at Williams, Amherst, Dartmouth, and Mount Holyoke before he came to Boston University in 1940. Two sons, Charles Loring and Gerald Warner, and a daughter, Barbara, were born to their union and the blessing of five grandchildren was known before Brace died.

Huldah was born in New York in 1902 and shortly afterwards her family moved to Jamaica Plain, a Boston suburb. Her father was the head of the Boston Classical School and also principal of Roxbury High School. Huldah's mother was proud of her Vermont heritage. Her daughter was graduated from Boston University (College of Liberal Arts) in 1925 and was a biology instructor for two years at Lasell Seminary just before her marriage to Gerald Brace. Their marriage to all appearances had the kind of stability and graciousness that the reader of *Days That Were* might expect; or, to put it another way for those who have read *The Department,* the Brace marriage appears to have nothing in common with that of Robert and Harriet Sanderling except that both of these professors specialized in the English novel.

Brace evidently had a gift for friendships, as *Days That Were* illustrates. Yet he was no seeker of the social or literary limelight. His life, one might easily assume, had been taken up largely with his writing interests along with his full-time teaching commitments. Let the following quotation serve to indicate both the essential modesty of the author as well as to outline what has been a truly productive life:

I was once a scholar and teacher, a writer of novels, a painter of pictures, a sailor and boat designer, a trout fisherman, a skier and climber, a carpenter, and handyman, a father and husband—and there seemed to be no end to the hours and days and years at my disposal, or the effort I could spend on them. Yet actually my enterprises are not comparable to those of the great ones of the world—of my grandfather, for example—and seem to me quite desultory and self-indulgent. I had on the whole very good luck, more than I ever really deserved. (p. 153)

For the rest it would be wise, I believe, to turn to a consideration of the novels that were written by Gerald W. Brace, and let them help to complete our impression of the man.

CHAPTER 2

Two Early Novels

IN 1969 Gerald Brace, looking back and remembering the literary scene in America when he began to write fiction, wrote in his book *The Stuff of Fiction:*

When I first read Mr. Gorman's commentary (on Joyce's *Portrait*) some thirty-five years ago, I made a pencilled note in the margin: "nonsense"—one word. It seemed to me then, in the late twenties and after, that the potentials of fiction were infinite. I felt the great adventure of it. James and Hardy and Conrad had just done splendid deeds, as had Lawrence and Hemingway and Faulkner, and the toughminded naturalists like Dreiser. The world was opening up and beckoning as it never had before. Lewis had discovered Main Street from coast to coast. Dos Passos took in the whole U.S.A. Farrell occupied the streets of Chicago, Steinbeck the dust bowl. The novel, especially the American novel, was filled with the strength and energy of a great age of exploration.[1]

Herbert Gorman had written in 1926 that all novelists must now come under Joyce's influence. I think Brace's response to Gorman provides a good focal point at which to begin to reflect on Brace's own production of fiction. Certainly writers of diversified backgrounds and interests were struggling to express their vision. Brace indeed was living in and beginning to produce his stories in an American artistic milieu which was varied and dynamic.

The Brace novels (with the slight exceptions of parts of *A Summer's Tale*, 1949) have not, however, been concerned with America at the business of war. He belongs to a between-the-wars generation and his novels develop out of his experience in New England living and in teaching English in several different colleges there. Nor does his fiction tend to be directly concerned with the large social disorders and struggles over labor, politics or religion. This is not to say, however, that violent and radical social changes occurring in the early and middle years of the author's life are not reflected in his fiction. For the most part his narratives parallel in their social settings and milieu what the reader at least guesses might be something like the general life experience of the author himself. Occasionally (notably in *The Garretson Chronicle,* 1947) a major portion of the novel moves back into the chronicle of the hero's family but mostly the novels center on the progress of the hero in a contemporary context.

Possibly since he is a novelist of New England and of those locales in New England that are not so much associated with social upheaval in the middle years of the twentieth century as other regions, his writing contains less of the sensational than what readers have come to associate with the novels of our time. Perhaps it should be put more positively. Sarah Orne Jewett counseled her good friend Willa Cather about experience and writing. Her advice was that a person should come to know the world of larger experience before coming to write about the village. And granting that the ways of artistic development and of the creative process are infinitely various, there is a general truth in Miss Jewett's remarks. I think it can be ascertained from even a first reading of Mr. Brace's first novel, *The Islands* (1936), that he is a writer of some depth, one who is conscious of the issues of the age in which he lives and writes, and that his novels, while chronicling New England life with a fine authenticity, are at the same time concerned with the rest of the world as well, with all the social forces that bear upon men and women wherever they reside. In short, Gerald Brace early in his career gives evidence that he is not merely writing of the parochial scene but of the world.

I   The Islands

The narrative is divided into five roughly equal segments, the last four of which chart the emotional growth of young Edgar Thurlow from boyhood to manhood when he is given an unexpected opportunity for a university education after the sudden death by drowning of his fisherman father. The opening section captures the harsh beauty of existence on the offshore islands of eastern Maine. John Thurlow returns home after many months at sea on a merchant vessel. He rows through the dark coastal waters to call on an old friend, Sarah Green. Her warm, unsophisticated greeting of John bespeaks a tacit agreement about marriage. The story moves quickly from this October reunion to an April wedding. The two come back to live on Moose Island, on the seaward end, where the Thurlows built their own home over ninety years before, with its garden and its orchard between the woods and the sea. John had gone to sea at eighteen and had in eight years become a mate on a barkentine. He and Sarah were settling down now to live mainly by catching the sea herring, the haddock, the cod, and the lobster and selling them to the canneries:

There was no change in life, except for the changing seasons. The winter coming, the winter going, the pleasantness of summer, were the events marking the year—but mostly before and after, for the actuality seemed to come imperceptibly. The weather was dominant over all thought, all speech, all of the life itself and even if he were doing nothing better than splitting stovewood, a man must anxiously sniff the slant of the wind and eye the distant streaks of fog on the headlands of the outer island. But a man had a wide horizon; he did variable and venturesome work; weather of the outer islands was relevant. A woman existed only in her kitchen.[2]

First came Linette and then a year and a half later came Edgar; the third child died in infancy. For neighbors there were the Crocketts and their three boys who lived up the road. And that "grim knot of a man" Rupe Brown who taught the boys how to handle fish. And there was old Granny Sue Todd who lived in a cottage with her grandson. Granny Sue would not bother with the boys' teasing as she passed by them in the woods. She would merely mumble and fasten her eyes on the ground looking for berries.

Sarah Thurlow "lived half imprisoned, in constant tension, worried a little at the necessity of life." But as the years passed along somehow Sarah learned to live a little more easily with her stoical husband, John. The reticent Edgar, about to enter high school, would much rather wield an axe to help stack the winter's supply of cordwood or to help mend the lobster traps for his father. The author gives the reader a fair view of the movement of life on the island in this opening segment of the novel.

Part II concerns two major events in the life of Edgar Thurlow now the central focus in the novel. Harvard Professor Everett, his wife, and his spinster sister, Nancy, buy a section of Thurlow's point and build a cottage there. A perennial attraction to the Boston social set, the Maine Coast provided among other relaxations the escape from hay fever. With the Everetts is also a young collegian, Jane Banks, who becomes a good friend of Edgar's. When the Everetts leave in the fall, Aunt Nancy remains on Moose Island.

Tragedy strikes the Thurlow family. Sarah watches for the return of her husband and son from the day's fishing. The launch returns with Edgar only aboard. Edgar, separated from his father, who was in the tender, hadn't even seen John disappear into the choppy waters. Nancy Everett, aging spinster and social worker, "conceived an idea and a vision." She would help educate Edgar Thurlow by putting him through Harvard. Sarah Thurlow is talked into the plan without much opposition. She will go to Herring Island and keep house for Mose Green, her widowed brother and tend to his five children, a rather bleak prospect for herself. Edgar at thirteen "felt himself trivial. He atoned for his share of the tragedy by not questioning, by being as passive as possible."

Edgar's advent at the Beacon Street home of Nancy Everett brings natural complications. The youngster bristles at the social gatherings; he rebels at the delicacy of the table manners. He is entered in mid-term at a Huntington Avenue private school. He answers a society matron's question about his well being: "Well I guess I feel like hell." Jane Banks tries to ease things by sidetrips to the South Shore. Nancy Everett perceives the boy needs a different kind of school, a chance to work with some tools. Edgar disappears. He turns up at Gloucester with an Italian family where he has become enamoured of their fishing craft, *The Rose*. As things turn out Edgar's infatuation is also for *The Rose's* namesake, Rose Fucci, "dusky face, flushed, blackbrowed, beautiful and just slightly older than Edgar."

Images of Gloucester and Rose Fucci haunt his adolescent mind the rest of the winter. In a major scene in the novel, Edgar is invited to go on a family reunion trip on *The Rose* with the Fuccis. Edgar manages to get drunk on a glass of Italian wine as he tries to keep his eye on Rose as the ship moves across the harbor. Rose has other admirers and gives her attentions impartially to all. Edgar returns to Boston feeling Rose was one only to dream of. He returns to Herring Island, greets his mother quietly and looks forward to working on boats with his uncle, Mose Green.

Part III of *The Islands* intensifies the internal conflict. Edgar transfers to Weston Academy to better prepare for Harvard. Later he goes abroad with Nancy Everett and on his return gets into Harvard as a junior in Engineering. When he returns to Moose Island for Christmas the issue of his future is critically focused. Mose Green offers him a chance to go into a boat-building partnership on Moose Island where the tourist trade has been developing. His mother counts herself unfit to offer advice to a college man but speaks to her son about his mediocre grades: "If you don't get on so well, you'd better stick to it." Nancy Everett is understanding but advises finishing his course.

Part IV ends with another love episode. Through the Everetts Edgar met Joan Lathrop, a graduate student at Radcliffe, who has a hobby of building model ships. She insinuates herself into Edgar's life, playing upon his interests in things nautical. She is somewhat attractive, but essentially flaccid and effete; and Edgar at first resists her advances. On a trip to the Cape with Nancy Everett as chaperone, Joan maneuvers Edgar aside on a scrubby bit of island and makes all the advances: "Edgar could not help taking her then. But the compulsion was strange, the fascinating predicament had caught him unprepared, snatching him so abruptly out of his range of experience that he fumbled blindly. He was conscious of sin . . . she was not Joan to him. Her smile pitied him and encouraged him to come up to her level of happiness. But he failed."[3]

The final segment of the story occurs at Moose Island during the summer before Edgar's final year at Harvard. He accidentally meets with Isabel Allen, the daughter of a minister on the island. Isabel's appearance—pink-faced, blue-eyed, braided hair—belie her twenty-one years. Edgar is enchanted and finds Isabel's image crowding his thoughts as he happily works with Mose Green to finish construction of a schooner for the fall. Joan Lathrop, still maneuvering for Edgar, comes with her uncle for a visit with the Everetts. She tries desperately to win Edgar in a last meeting with him, but he cannot return her affection. She is reported drowned shortly afterwards, and no trace is found of her after several days' search.

Jane Banks and Nancy Everett unsuccessfully entreat Edgar to return to Harvard. Edgar has made his decision to build his future on what he loves best—building boats. Edgar's swift and fervent pursuit of Isabel is turned away. She takes his kisses with warmth but refuses any commitment because she feels inexperienced in romance. But there are some final hints given that a possibility at least remains for Isabel's later return to Edgar.

II   *Brace and Jewett*

The Country of the Pointed Firs by Sarah Orne Jewett comes to mind as dealing with the same ambience as Brace's *The Islands,* most especially in the first two sections of the novel where the quiet and somewhat grim life of the Island people is delineated. Their houses are settled along the water's edge. The folk are hardy individualists who come to know early that the earth and the sea, although they promise much, do not often, if ever, fulfill their promises. Recollect Miss Jewett's Elmira Todd's holding her secret of disappointed love. When she married she knew it could not be the thing that might have made her most happy, and even in her limited happiness her lover is lost at sea after a brief period. Similarly, Sarah Thurlow enters marriage with John with a sense of duty but also with some desire for happiness. With the early loss of a husband the world of Moose Island offers little else than a lonesome existence and a chance to help others.

Both Brace and Jewett are aware of the meager opportunities offered to the people that lived by the sea, but they also know that these folk have been bred to the idea that one had to live out one's allotted span the best way one could and that meant often turning to one's neighbors and enduring with them a common fate. The pennyroyal which Elmira Todd constantly seeks in the Jewett masterpiece is part of her livelihood, but more importantly it is a symbol of her ties with the community. Hers certainly is not the profit motive. She knows which herbs are likeliest to help clients the most and her search for them is constant.

Jewett's world of Dunnet Landing is older by several generations than the community of Brace's Thurlow's Cove, where modern equipment of all sorts is coming to be used in the building of boats and houses. Pleasure crafts are more in demand by the vacationers than fishing boats, but the local people are not so subject to change. It is clear that neither Brace nor Miss

Jewett sees these coastal folk as sexual aberrants in the way some modern analysts might. While there are, in Miss Jewett's stories, characters such as the hermitess of Shell Island and William Todd (who needs just about a lifetime to propose to Esther and take her from her lonely existence), there are many more people whose lives are very ordinary. Sexual differences do distinguish the books, however. Miss Jewett's world is sometimes compared with the *Cranford* of Elizabeth Gaskell wherein the woman's point of view necessarily prevails, since their sex is so predominant in that English village, a fact caused by a major shifting of economic forces in England. Brace's story *The Islands* largely contrasts with Miss Jewett's representations in its strong, masculine sense. Brace, however, has sympathy for the greater hardships which the women faced, as when the sea claimed a father or a son. Both writers of the Maine coast share an intense love of the seasons. *The Islands* celebrates a man's dedication to craftsmanship (as do most of the other Brace novels). The more nervous people are apt to be those who live in the city. The Maine folk are found more "normal" in their basic idiosyncracies, their tragedies and their occasional triumphs.

Arthur S. Harris, Jr., writing in *College English,* makes some shrewd assessments of Brace's writing up through *Bell's Landing* (1955). He sees *The Islands*—accurately, I believe—as containing a good many of the qualities that have made Brace a novelist of worth. He finds that Brace is a careful writer, a meticulous composer of sentences, one who scarcely in his whole canon can be convicted of syntactical imperfection. Harris's second point is that the pace of the Brace novels, especially the earlier ones, is so leisurely that Harris questions whether the reader is not in danger of being stalled at certain points. But he rightly, I think, points out that the reader is being invited often to savor, for example, a seascape or to enjoy the particular shading of the sunlight playing upon a house along a Back Bay street. Finally, Harris characterizes Brace's writing as purveying "an indefinite sense of time"—possibly, the critic infers, because the novelist is seeking to get a "measure of timelessness" into the stories.[4] Hence while readers of *The Islands* easily follow the changing environment of Edgar's life they might have to pause to ask themselves just when in the early part of the twentieth century these events were occurring.

In 1963 in a talk at Amherst College Gerald W. Brace said

several significant things about the wellsprings of his novelistic career. He talked mainly about hiking over the hills of Massachusetts, New Hampshire, and Vermont and the influence it had upon his later career. It is worthwhile to record what he has to say about *The Islands,* even though he seems to be discrediting it to some extent:

My first novel, *The Islands,* appeared some twelve years after my graduation. A Maine coast story with Boston interludes, but the beginnings of it go back to Professor Whicher's writing seminar where I was encouraged to work on the Maine material; the twelve years represent error and failure and the discouraging effort to put into practice the lessons I had been taught. A writer's judgment of his own books is of no value, but I suppose *The Islands* is implicitly romantic and transcendental and full of an enthusiasm that may have vanished from my life. Shades of the prison house, as Wordsworth says, "do close about us as we grow old."[5]

Robert P. Tristram Coffin, an expert writer about New England himself who reviewed Brace's first novel in the *New York Herald Tribune,* sensed very well that

these men and women Gerald Brace writes about get a good deal of their nature from the place. Summer people come to Maine for a change. And they succeed in finding one. They find themselves in a new world among these balsams and in this low light, among trees and people as remote from Beacon Street as a border ballad. They find bedrock living on bedrock islands. And it is as refreshing as coming on a cold spring in the midst of July. Life can look good when pared down to bare essentials of food and work and sleep. . . . The emptiness that has suddenly opened up before the feet of prosperous nations since 1900 probably has something to do with Edgar Thurlow's return to his islands. But the moral lies deeper than that. There is a notion of the old American independence of spirit here. A lot of the everlasting toughness of the Puritan creed. Edgar returns to his small world mainly because men still feel the need of loneliness and will return to find in it themselves.[6]

Brace was surprised at Coffin's words of tribute for his novel. Later he also thought that S. O. Jewett's book was not a large influence on his own novel because he had not yet come to know it that well.

The Islands is a novel that aims at realism, despite Brace's own words about its romanticism. The book draws its modest symbols from the very texture of Maine coastal life, as needed, to reinforce the narrative. And since this same life has so much to do with the ocean, it is not surprising that the prevailing symbols are nautical ones. There is the humble fishing boat of the Thurlows plying the waters of the cove; there is the more splendid craft, Rose, of the Fuccis from Gloucester; there is the significantly ineffectual life of Joan Lathrop reflected in her tinkering with ship models; and finally there is the polished new yacht produced by Edgar's craftsmanship. An ordinary life of a young man is chronicled with an intensive honesty by Brace and this makes the story worthwhile. The author labors to assist the reader's sense perceptions to form a clear image of Edgar Thurlow's life.

Yet of course *The Islands* inevitably reveals the defects of any first novel. One very important factor was simply that the novel took ten years to bring to completion. Brace had begun it in graduate school creative writing classes and had revised it several times. He never was a writer of more than three or four hundred words a day even in later phases of his career, and during this early period he was handicapped by the tasks of completing graduate school and starting to earn his living as a college teacher at a time when employment was difficult to obtain.

This interruption in the writing of the book shows primarily I believe, in the unevenness of narrative pace. The reader sees the growth of Edgar's youth in a too steady progression of incidents which might have been varied in their patterning. There are frequent contrasts of city life with Edgar's return to the coastland but these tend to become too measured and too frequent.

In assessing Brace's overall vision of life from his first effort as novelist it becomes clear, I believe, that he was taking an honest but a loving look at people who were quietly and faithfully struggling to make the best of their destinies. Most of them were living in the same world their fathers and grandfathers had lived in. But the author could not be said to be representing them as backward. On the other hand Edgar Thurlow clearly is well on his way to becoming a more substantial person in the coastal community because he combines his native talents with the social and educational experience.

Brace assumes no apparent philosophical or religious stance in this first book, as he sets about to delineate the manner of life which he finds in various parts of New England with its Puritan roots. Perhaps the Jamesian dictum of "felt life" is a good phrase to muster at this point. There are no topical allusions to date the action of the novel but the general tone gives off the flavor of early twentieth-century life in America, pre-World War I. Thus Brace's writing is not easily allied to the dominant fictional themes of the time as garnered, say from Hemingway or Faulkner or Steinbeck. However, in the progress of Edgar Thurlow's young life there is certainly a sense of a world that is changing significantly around the hero. And ultimately this adjustment that Edgar Thurlow makes is not essentially different from that of Nick Adams or perhaps of Jody Tiflin in Steinbeck's *The Red Pony*. In this respect the ending of the novel indicates clearly that for Edgar the primary values are grounded in an honest relationship with other people. He must finally disappoint Miss Everett's hopes about his degree in order that he may be himself and build his boats. To follow Brace's reading of the New England character in its various manifestations and locations is one of the main purposes of this study.

III   The Wayward Pilgrims

There's a kind of story where the reader steadily anticipates a great revelation. Maybe *Pilgrim's Progress* is one, but we'd handle it differently now; we'd put in a new twist and surprise the reader by omitting the revelation entirely. The moral, of course, is that life does it too—or so we think. Much preparation, much expectation, and then—nothing; irony.

The Wayward Pilgrims

Mr. Brace's second novel, *The Wayward Pilgrims* (1938), was published two years after *The Islands*. It is a loosely structured narrative of a young Harvard graduate student on a study grant who travels into Vermont and meets up with an older woman. The setting is again New England; this time the focus is the mountains and the people of Vermont. It is different from any other story that Brace would write. Jorge Luis Borges has written that there is a little of the allegorist in every novelist and it might appear, at least at first consideration, that some allegory was surfacing in this second novel. However, in a conversation with the writer of this book the novelist declined to attribute any such conscious design to *The Wayward Pilgrims.*

The Islands had grown naturally enough out of the author's long association with Maine folk as well as out of the atmosphere of city and school life. This second novel reflects, Brace tells us, many treks that he had made, especially while he was an undergraduate at Amherst becoming more interested in the pursuit of actual life than in the curriculum mapped out by the professors. He tramped along Vermont dirt roads, listening to country accents and dialects, in pleasant and rough weather. He had gone over mountains familiar to skiers (Killington, Equinox, and Stratton) in search mainly of those things that make the Yankee native what he is. Even as an Amherst freshman, the hills about the college were to him "like the call of distant bugles." It was the real beginning for him of his writing career in the sense that he followed that music as he explored first the Pelham Hills, Mount Toby, and Mount Lincoln. A year later he extended his explorations to the New Hampshire villages of New Salem and Conway and to the top of Monadnock.[7] Of course roughing it had been a life that his father had introduced him to thoroughly in his youth when they explored eastern and northern Maine, going over some of the territory that Thoreau wrote about in his volume *The Maine Woods.*

Brace saw it later as a learning process and looked back on those days with a certain fondness:

But I met many people, ate and slept in many strange places, listened to voices, took note of old stories and old ways, observing lumbering operations in winter and sugaring in early spring. Some of those I met were defeated and discouraged by poverty and stony soil, but men carried on with the moral courage of their great tradition; they worked their farms as hard as they could, lived in clean houses, and welcomed the young stranger with humor and good will and ancient courtesy.

The Wayward Pilgrims opens with the central figure of the story, Lawrence Minot, in a trancelike mood and situation. He is working in the library of Harvard University, faithfully taking notes on Burke and his notion of the sublime, in the final stages of preparation for the writing of his Ph.D. theses. But it is April in Boston and Minot is "overshadowed by the dreams of things." He shakes himself to his senses and banishes his thoughts about the dour old professor Wadsworth and his everlasting insistence on detail and his equally strong lack of anything meaningfully human. Minot's soul is revived by his running the four miles along the river bank back to his quarters. Later he gets unexpected news that he has received a university grant of $300 for American language research. He decides to accept the grant and postpone the four month task of writing his thesis. He will pursue the "gleam" or "destiny," as he confides facetiously to his roommate. He will go on a walking tour into the Green Mountains, justifying his existence as the prospective scholar (which he hardly takes seriously) by recording some of the phenomena of Yankee speech.

First he encounters Mary Butterfield on the train north. Minot engages her in conversation, but she makes him somewhat uneasy with her straight talk about her Vermont background. She has enough sophistication to meet Minot on his own terms. She explains she is trying to help her folks save the homestead and to decide about marriage with her young man. Mary provides the story with the first of Brace's portraits of varied Vermonters. She comes to represent, like Jane Banks in *The Islands,* a girl who is very well balanced, reflecting values derived from the necessity of growing up in a family where interdependence and mutual support are the common mode. The scene provides a significant introduction to Vermont life.

Minot gets off the train at Redfield. As he is eating lunch at the station he encounters Margot, a woman of indeterminate age "between twenty-five and forty." She has lost her purse as she was enroute from the town of Peru, Vermont (about sixty miles north) to Chicago. Minot learns a while later that she had decided that morning to leave her artist husband and had taken what little money there was available. As Minot first becomes aware of the woman's presence she seems vaguely symbolic: "Duessa, the embodiment of all evil, a woman of darkness. He grinned at his folly. . . ."

Minot is cautious about any involvement. The two meet again at a small bridge near the edge of town. Margot has decided to head back again to her husband in the mountains. The two find they have a common direction and their mutual honesty with each other helps Margot admit she had lingered at the bridge to tell Minot her story. And Minot admits he had questioned her innocence. Thus begins the relationship between two pilgrims which will encompass four days and nights.

Margot refuses any money from her companion. She gradually unfolds her past. She has been married three times. First, when she was twenty-one to George, whom she left when he turned into "a righteous Male Republican with old fashion virtues." Clearly Margot is a diminished Alice of Bath figure in the modern world, a woman who has been around, one who carries on the struggle the best way she can. The two pilgrims head northeast, admiring the early May beauty. "Nature's first green is gold" was Frost's way of putting it and Minot's thoughts and words frequently contain echoes of the famous New England poet. For example, Minot observes, "There's something about the way things look. . . . The leaves are all golden. You can see way off through there where the light shimmers like mist. You could walk in those woods."

Such talk of nature, reflecting Frostian tones, is generally well orchestrated throughout the book. It helps to deliver the subtle emotional nuances that Brace is aiming for in the development of the two main characters of the novel. As in "West Running Brook" the dramatic monologue of Robert Frost manages skillfully to bring out the essential difference in the masculine and feminine psyches of the two lovers, so Brace at least in a modulation that suits his situation in this novel manages to draw out character by the interplay of dialogue and observations upon the natural beauty of the Vermont landscape. A stone Civil War monument of a soldier on the village green stimulates talk of man himself "still undiscovered." Minot feels that the statue, unappreciated by the townsmen, is perhaps no worse than the Sargent murals in the Harvard library. The soldier for Minot is a character such as Eugene O'Neill's Brigadier General Ezra Mannon in *Mourning Becomes Electra* or a hero of another O'Neill play come home to find himself in the terrible complexity of a family war. Minot's pondering over the statue stirs Margot to compare the figure to her current artist husband, Mike, who sees a grim Yankee storekeeper and goes home to paint him as if he is "either incestuous or half-witted or both, and it's his duty to paint that and nothing else."

As Minot drifts into a deeper interest in his companion he is fairly uncertain as to how he should be handling the situation. He is definitely attracted to the dark-haired, white-skinned woman walking beside him. He realizes that for the past several years he had not really been engaged in life and here is life walking now

with him. Minot is familiar with Chaucer's famous wayfarer from
Bath and with the Elizabethan comedies and their morality, too.
But due to his upbringing by his Unitarian minister as father he
had postponed any relationship with woman and led a sheltered
life. The hour grows late as they come to a tiny village of Pagan
Hill. Before the evening closes in on them Margot tells of her
second marriage. She had become a taxi-dancer on Broadway
and got involved in rescuing Pete from a gun fight with the
police after he was wounded. She finds herself living with Pete.
"How would you put it? Professional woman? — you've got to put
the accent on woman. That sounds as though I was calling myself
a prostitute, but I wasn't technically. Nearly all women have
talents of that sort, and it's hard to put labels on them. The big
difference is that some are honest about it and some aren't."
Margot and Pete got along, especially on their camping
weekends on Greylock, and they married later and started a
family. The infant died in the womb after Pete was murdered.
His former partner sold out his business to a mob and Pete
resisted.

The two pilgrims arrive in an old sugarhouse on a hillside.
They find inside old Mr. Shattuck who offers them the use of the
crude lodging. His "hi-yah" conveys something "midway between a laugh and a sigh." Margot lies by the fire Mr. Shattuck
rekindles in the sugaring-off stove; Minot sleeps nearer the wall
and old Mr. Shattuck in the corner.

The next morning Minot wakes early and walks up the hillside,
meditating among the silver trees, enjoying the maple woods and
the flowers. He hears the song of the hermit thrush "beyond a
curtain of sun-drawn mist, and Minot pausing and lifting his head
knew he would never come closer to the revelation." It is a
moment of quiet and muted epiphany for Lawrence Minot. Again
one is reminded of the similarity of Frost's famous lyrics which
evoke the mystery of trees and the edge of wooded areas. He
continues his morning climb to the hilltop which enables him to
see the mountains to the north "cold and distant reaching away
into eternity. South was where you come from."

The loose narrative journey motif of *The Wayward Pilgrims*
gives the author a chance to explore the natural setting and
Brace renders it very meaningfully to the story throughout. It
accounts largely for the charm of a book whose action does not
provide much for the reader's ordinary expectations of suspense.

For the reader who becomes interested in such unfolding of
landscape the novel does provide many insights into the author's
conceptions of life and his sense of values, as in this passage when
Minot is up on the mountain looking down upon the sugarhouse:

Wood smoke came from the small stove pipe in the sugarhouse, a
fragrant clean smoke that hung like a blue curtain on the trees. The
scene stopped him again, the little amber house settled against the
hillside, the high silver-gray trees, the brook and the dark young
hemlocks along it. There was something in the angles of the house, the
bit of raised roof like a low cupola where the steam came out, the
slanting shed over the sap tank on the north side against the hill, the
woodshed open to the sun—something that touched the pit of his
stomach, like the lines of a good painting, like the phrase of music
beautiful beyond reason. It was a kind of finality, like all great beauty.
Color and form and meaning—as far as one could ever tell about
meaning—had composed themselves into one thing.[8]

Reflecting on this novel in later years, Brace disclaimed
wisdom "in any classic sense" or "profundities" for his early
novel, but he did affirm that "the gleams and glimpses of life, of
farms and villages and mountain roads and the folk who lived
there, all seen in the eyes of a romantic young scholar, were as
authentic as I could make them."[9] Such a glimpse in the above
excerpt has a genuineness about it. And it points towards the kind
of beauty that is incorporated into Brace's later writing. It
combines simple, effective rendering of the external with an
inward awareness of the protagonist which the reader may
share.

Margot and Lawrence continue northward. She is a sensitive
respondent to his observations. He sees her essentially as a truth
seeker, just as he is. Margot wonders if all the modern desolation
couldn't be accounted for by a lovely allegory, i.e., the farmer
leaves his green acres on Pagan Hill, pushing his wife and
children westward, always pursuing the golden vision and letting
the old homestead go into ruins. But she concludes that one can
not make a satisfactory allegory out of life, not even her own as
an illustration of the seven deadly sins. She seems to be implicitly
asking that Minot not judge her too harshly.

Mr. Shattuck accompanies the two pilgrims a brief way. His
life story is succinctly interpolated into the narrative. He was
married for thirty years and chose to live on the mountain farm

when his wife died. His sons began to insist on a housekeeper for him, which led to an unsuccessful second marriage with a woman who already had a grown boy.

Next thing we was getting married and payin' for a new car . . . a slow spreading smile came into his face as the idea worked towards the surface; he opened his mouth and nodded to them several times. "Them first few months" he said at last, "she was sweet: sweet as maple cream." Then he laughed silently and said "hi-yah" with an audible chuckle that was half a sigh.[10]

In the sadness of Mr. Shattuck and yet, in his basic human friendliness, the novel catches at the central grain of the Vermont life. He is the local historian, who points out the old walls and shells of cellars that were once a part of a thriving community. One does not have to point out the many resemblances in the book to those scenes familiar to so many readers of Frost's *North of Boston*. When the talk of the three turns to death and immortality, Minot and Margot confess to Shattuck no particular faith in heaven. Shattuck seems hesitant to express his own innermost feelings. "It don't make so much difference." For Margot Old Shattuck is the kind of man that upsets her allegory. If the old Vermonter had gone west he would have gone merely for the going.

The second night for the two pilgrims is spent in a farmhouse where they become the guests of a farmer and his wife who receive them very reluctantly. Wearied from their walk they spend the night in a single room with its single bed outfitted with greasy cotton blankets. Their hosts, wanting the money, had not made any enquiries that would embarrass. Lawrence begins to fumble for words to express his beginning love. He feels that he and Margot are one person in their friendship. Margot gently puts him off, saying that "every woman begins by being someone else — until you get to know her." The two share the lumpy bed — but not each other, Margot going to sleep from fatigue and Minot lying on the edge of his side of the bed.

The pilgrim's third day contains some more insights into Margot's past. Prostitution was a possible alternative she considered open to her to escape the drudgery of being a waitress in New York after her husband was killed in gang war, "but even a good body isn't worth what it used to be . . . the idea that sin is a glamorous escape to be paid for later is just storybook stuff. Professional sin as far as I could ever find out is inhumanly stupid. . . . Maybe I don't know how it's done in the higher ranks, but I do know that giving the average New Yorker what he thinks is a good time is duller than an old-fashioned prayer meeting. You have to be very drunk before it even begins to seem faintly amusing."

Margot's present relationship with her third husband, Mike Anton, the artist, started out well enough, we learn. They had married in New York City and had left behind the sophistication of the art crowd to come to Vermont's mountains. For a brief period Mike's enthusiasm for life and for painting seemed rekindled. But he quite neglected Margot for the sake of the art, and a despair had overtaken him lately, which only his art alleviated.

When Lawrence finally makes a declaration of love to Margot it is done with directness, with a disclaiming of any power over words to express it and with great integrity of spirit. She puts off this declaration firmly be refusing to make any such return on her own. She offers herself to him, sexually—in a kind of gesture of her regard for him—if he so desires. Her unwillingness to give any commitment to the future seems to work against any further move. They kiss and the journey continues.

As the third night on the journey approaches, a storm darkens the valley in the region of Pike Mountain. They seek the shelter of a home in the village of Rockington. On this occasion they find a warm reception with the Carters. The two travelers make no disguise to the Carters of their actual status. They are accepted in turn as they are and sleep in separate rooms. In the simple but genuine richness of the Carter's home life the reader is made aware of significant values. An abundance of food is shared in a simple home which reflects people who know what they have sought in life and are modest and content in enjoying it in their late middle age. Minot feels that somehow the Carters have found an equilibrium in life, "an ease after toil and toil after ease." Nature is not subdued and neither is Matty Carter. However, he also feels that the secret the Carters have obviously found will be lost to the world for a long time.

In the morning when the storm had not quite abated Minot explores alone the neighboring mountain. As in the opening scene of the novel we find him jogging into the higher countryside, his energies at peak and his love for Margot occupying his thoughts. The whole scene is desolate, but as he returns he senses the processes of the rebirth of spring. His moment of supreme happiness was in his joining forces with the wind and the hills and the sky. The passage (from the chapter which is called "Purple Passage") is not overdone. The prose is just as effective as other similar but briefer passages of natural description.

Their fourth and final night is spent together in the hayloft of a barn which the two come upon when darkness once again overtakes them. At this time Margot is clearly desirous of giving herself to Minot. They spend the night as lovers and though Minot's heart is filled with great expectancy of the future, it is clear that Margot within herself feels they must soon part. It happens sooner than Minot expects. She is gone when he returns with food from the village. A few days later Minot is seen at the hillside home of Mike and Margot in Peru. There is a pencilled note for Minot from Margot on the door. Her artist husband has been lost, after wandering apparently aimlessly on the mountain during the storm. Lawrence learns later that Margot had stayed long enough to manage the husband's funeral but has left no forwarding address. The closing lines of the novel read: "He walked away. The eastward lowlands were swallowed in dusk; no mountains showed under the clouds. All that remained in the wide silent world was the gray road stretching away downward ahead of him."

There is a strong pastoral vein that runs through *The Wayward Pilgrims*. This second of the Brace novels is more impressionistic and its romanticism is lodged primarily in the conceptions of the young graduate student—a quiet yet perceptive incipient scholar who is being overtaken by life. He was the son of a Massachusetts minister; his life has been sheltered but he is neither naive essentially nor is he holding to any particular illusion. But he is given to philosophical reflection. His companion for the four days is more like him than she is different. That is to say, she questions life, will not accept its surface values and is perdurably honest in her relation to herself, her past and her friend.

The novel got mixed reviews. Frances Woodward in the *Atlantic* saw the work as "uneven, and without humor, but the good pages more than made up for the unfortunately literary bad ones."[11] The point about literariness refers to the Ph.D.

candidate Minot's frequent name-dropping of book titles, themes, and lines to Margot, during the course of their four-day walking trip into the hills and mountains of Vermont. Sometimes this habit seems to carry too much of a professorial tone. But at other times, it adds to the situation that is being developed. A sympathetic *Christian Science Monitor* reviewer claimed, on the other hand, that "although the plot itself was not probable" that other virtues of the story including its "luminous setting made the book very much worthwhile."[12]

B. H. Walter in the *New York Times* essentially wrote off *The Wayward Pilgrims* as a "pretentious and unsuccessful experiment." It was for him "unreal," "irritating," "tedious," although the use of landscape was nonetheless laudable. The heroine, Margot, was considered incredibly romantic. If the book did not altogether remove that critic's faith in the career of Brace, the novelist, it did not have "the quality of persuasive magic which it is obviously supposed to have."[13]

Finally, William Rose Benet saw the fiction in a more favorable light. "Mr. Brace avoids all sentimental pitfalls and yet imbues his book with the true beauty of possible relationships. There is something of the clean artistry of a Robert Nathan about this work, though his style is entirely his own."[14]

An essential question about the novel may be raised concerning the credibility of Margot. There is little doubt that the author wanted her seen as archetypically female. She is drawn to men and attracts men to herself. She has concern for other people. She sacrifices for them. She wants a home but ironically is destined to be on the road. Perhaps the nub of this issue is her quality of mind. For Minot she is attractive not only in body, but spiritually. She becomes a foil for him throughout the book as she responds to his philosophical questionings and in doing so she may not be so credible. The degree of literacy seen in her responses offers the reader's credibility no problem; it is rather the sustained nature of the philosophical exchanges between the two that does not bear long scrutiny. In general not only is the action of the novel, as seen through the eyes of the young student, properly called romantic, but essentially the novel itself is romantic in the sense that the fiction suggests an exploration of the author himself, in his own psychic landscapes, his searching of his own predispositions, his dreams, his illusions, if you will, all of which is not at all to say that Brace's own life was used as a basis for this novel except for the obvious familiarity with the Vermont terrain.

In the recent autobiography of his first twenty-one years, *Days That Were,* Mr. Brace speaks of the influence of Professor George Whicher of Amherst, who in his creative writing classes had used as one of his texts Hilaire Belloc's *The Path to Rome* (1902). Brace admits, in his account, a profound influence by this book which narrates how Belloc with his familiar exuberance makes a vow that he will travel on foot from his Alsatian home on a pilgrimage to Rome, stopping each morning of the more than seven-hundred-mile journey to go to morning Mass. What is unusual about the Belloc venture is that he traces a direct line between his point of departure and St. Peter's Basilica and vows that he will maintain such a route over the Alps. Belloc uses a breezy prose style to communicate freely to his readers his adventures along the way. Brace tells us how years later he went to Symphony Hall in Boston to hear Belloc lecture. It was a disillusioning experience in the sense that the Boston Catholic audience listened to a grim accounting by Belloc of the state of world affairs in which the *joie de vivre* of Belloc's adventurous early book was missing.[15] Despite his experience Brace still vigorously affirms the greatness of Belloc's adventure book and the literary lastingness of the shared experiences of the open road. And it is this same spirit, I think, which gives *The Wayward Pilgrims* its primary life, the joy of vagabondage caught in early youth and remembered and made into the stuff of fiction.

One still has to account for the antiromantic or heavily ironic ending of the novel. When Minot loses Margot there is a heavy gray shadowing of the experience. The exuberance which had marked the beginning of the trek into the mountains on the day of the storm and shortly before he had consummated his love with Margot, has now vanished with no traces of happiness. I conclude that on the whole the novel deserves to be called ironic-realistic as much as it deserves to be called romantic, in the final impression it leaves upon its readers.

I think the author himself is an important authority on the general scope and feeling of these first two novels. He says of them, in speaking to an Amherst College audience:

The world I discovered in and about Amherst certainly animates my books, if anything does. Even the alien settings of some of them, Boston and its surroundings, and the coast of Maine, are illuminated by what I learned in my Amherst years: The Vermont scenes in two of the novels (*The Wayward Pilgrims* and *The Light on a Mountain*) come into focus off there in the northwest, so many days hard walking over the back-country roads from Amherst, discovered originally and stored away in the pockets of memory by an errant student long ago. In most ways I had already belonged to New England, by heritage and habit, but until the Amherst experience I had no perspective over it, made no effort to see the truth of it. I was charged simply with a sort of transcendental eagerness; my heart was beguiled by mountains and valleys, islands and harbors, the solitude and wildness broken here and there by farm and village and steepled church. I knew the country and the coast as I had been taught to see them by the romantic poets, appareled in celestial light; and I suppose it was Amherst that added perspective and the beginnings of common sense to my dreams: not the college alone, nor my wise teacher, but the whole reality of life I began to share.[16]

Thus Gerald W. Brace in *The Wayward Pilgrims* widened his fictional investigation of the New England character and spirit. Perhaps he felt he was writing with something of the curiosity of those other writers who had been making similar inquiries. Robert Frost's explorations would seem, following the critical psychological ideas of William James, to have already opened up the New England territory that was then further exploited by Eugene O'Neill. Brace would add his own insights in the novels to come. And they would represent views, above all, honestly come by, views that grew out of his abiding interest in and love of New England people and their ways.

CHAPTER 3

Light on a Mountain

B RACE'S third novel appeared in 1941. The setting for this
story was similar to *The Wayward Pilgrims*—an area of
Stafford Mountain in southern Vermont, near Bellows Falls and
Brattleboro. But it was a very different kind of novel from the
second; a considerably larger canvas served to bring out Brace's
full capacities as storyteller. Instead of concentrating on the
quest of a particular young hero as in the first two novels, Brace
chose to focus upon a single year in the story of the Gaunts, a
family of Vermonters living on the slopes of Stafford Mountain in
the late 1930s.

I *The Mountain Family*

Like *The Islands,* the story is structured into four main
narrative segments, labeled "The Mountain," "Morton,"
"Sylvia," and "Twilight." The Gaunts are an old Vermont family.
They struggle in post-Depression America to gain a living from
their acreage by dairy farming on the mountainside where
sheepgrazing had once been the more characteristic occupation.
John and Carrie Gaunt have two sons, Morton and Henry, and a
younger daughter, Sylvia. Morton is twenty-three; Henry,
twenty-one; and Sylvia, seventeen. Morton is Mr. Gaunt's chief
"hand" around the farm and also one of his father's main
difficulties in life; Henry, finishing his third year at Wyndham
College, sixty miles away over the mountain, and Sylvia, about to
complete her high-school career, both have a poetic side to their
characters. They are far different from their free-wheeling
brother, Morton, a tough jack-of-all-trades intent on proving his
manhood to the community.

The novel opens on a note of direct conflict between Henry
and his father. Henry is annoyed by his father's selling the spruce

46

forest high up on Stafford Mountain. The buyers from Rutland
had stripped the land of the timber and laid waste the areas that
with their mossy glades and clear streams had provided Henry
with some delightful hours. When he got news of the sale he had
written a poem about it, published it in the college magazine, and
caused a stir in the English Department among the professors
about its merits. Henry's poetic inspiration for the moment came
from *The Waste Land*.

Neither Mr. Gaunt nor Morton shares any of Henry's poetic
sensibilities. They jibe him about his interests while Henry
performs his share of the farm chores. Morton had barely made it
through high school, a boorish Brom Bones of the community.
But he was a hard worker and skilled. Henry, too, works with
vigor—putting a new roof on the shed, milking cows, or mending
walls.

Sylvia Gaunt, with her sylphlike personality, has a natural
bond of sympathy with her poetic brother. She, too, revels in the
out-of-doors, mountain-climbing and skiing. An early, major
episode concerns Sylvia's efforts at a prize contest for speaking.
Characteristically she has neglected to prepare a speech on an
assigned topic but turns her impromptu talk into an indictment of
Vermont provincialism and comes off with first place. Similarly
at graduation, her poem "Green Mountain Interval" (with its title
freely borrowed from Robert Frost) continues her theme of
probing into life with a freshness that her brother finds
admirable ("Under the trees the dirt is lean / Under the dirt our
bones are clean"). Henry sees in her verses something he can
take a lesson from; he wants to get away from the modern school
of wasteland cynics.

Mrs. Carrie Gaunt defends both Sylvia's and Henry's individualism against Mr. Gaunt's charge of craziness. She reminds him
that her own mother was the kind that would delay supper to do
some flower gathering and that the home life was happier for it.
Like Henry she tries to recognize that there are different natures
and she sees her own as that of a "practical body" who can't ever
neglect her household duties.

The action of Part I climaxes when the Gaunts awaken one
midsummer morning to find themselves being introduced to
Morton's bride, Marjie, with whom no one in the house has had
the slightest acquaintance. She is a new girl to the village who

had been living with her aunt and uncle. For Carrie the marriage is a great shock. She tries to counter it by turning the house inside out with her cleaning, showing in her face "The conviction of despair and unbearable pain". Quickly it becomes apparent that the Gaunt household has acquired a helpless young female whose sole interest in life is centered on going to town to dance or to shop.

Morton's basic coarseness and rudeness show in his speaking about his hastily acquired bride. He confronts Henry for an opinion and gets it: "Well, I tell you Morton—you think I am a damned fool and I think you're a damned fool and there we are . . . you seem to think it's funny to make 'em suffer. . . . If you had any sense you'd know a shock like this has half killed them." In their actions Henry and Sylvia make sincere attempts to make Marjie feel welcome in the mountain home.

In the final pages of this first section of the story Henry hikes up the mountain to clear his mind of the turmoil. When Henry comes down the westward slope in late afternoon he comes upon a deserted farm deep in overgrowth of grass and weed. "The fierce blaze of western sun behind flashed on the windows and threw blue shadows up the slopes behind. Gray shingled roof and wall washed in rich light, emerald grass of the yard emerging in the tawny fields—soon it would fall in ruin and disaster, but just now it stood up with a quaint sort of pride all firm and clean. The deepening night gave it a character like a painting, with focused meaning; you saw at a glance its forlorn dwindling strength, you felt the bulk of the mountain behind and the windy ocean of space in front" (p. 83).[1]

This rendering of the neighboring deserted farmhouse, whose occupants Henry had known from his boyhood, is in the style of Willa Cather's well-known prairie image of the ploughshare caught within the orb of the setting sun in *My Ántonia*. It strongly stands out among other less evocative scenes in *Light On The Mountain* and it gains meaning as the novel goes along. The farm had been lived in by Martha Sargent in her old age. She stayed on for fifteen years after her husband left her for his dream of an easy life and dancing girls in the South Pacific. Now Henry approaches the windows and peers in to observe the kitchen things that looked somehow diminished from what he remembers. As he leaves he looks back and feels that he had seen a ghost in "the fire-like gleam of sun from a window. . . .

"It seemed unreasonable that he should have to search for truth; other people didn't—his brother Morton, and all those who went ahead strongly with life. Perhaps it wasn't truth anyway so much as self-justification, an expression of fear. He backed in against the mountains, retreating from hostility, holding to what he felt to be forever secure, taking strength from native earth" (pp. 85–86). Henry Gaunt sees himself as one with his mother, driving in the horse and buggy up to Martha Sargent's place, and one with desperate old Martin Sargent with his bad dream of the South Seas, and one with all the Gaunts and other mountain folk. He descends the mountain forgiving his father for the destruction of the sprucelands. Henry now appears ready to test the rest of the world—to measure its differences with life on Stafford Mountain.

Section II of the novel is basically a flashback into Morton's earlier life, comprising chiefly an interpolated tale of how at fifteen he singlehandedly brought in an escaped convict who had been menacing the whole countryside. Morton (still in grade school at fifteen) knew about Lecka, who had hid in the Sargent cabin on one occasion. The event had much to do with the shaping of Morton's personality. It began when Morton had started to run around with a group of boys his own age and one slightly older lad. They concocted a scheme against Morton—to give him a hiding and leave him naked and painted red. The plan almost works. Morton salvages his trousers and vows individual revenge.

Morton's capture of the escapee takes the edge off his planned revenge. Like a youthful Deerslayer Morton knows the woods intimately and figures out where the convict may be hiding. He receives no encouragement from his family or even the state troopers in the venture as he tracks down Lecka in an old sugar house. Morton's account of the capture obscures the real fear and also the aggression he had felt. But the incident boosts his ego. This episode ends with a father-son clash: Mr. Gaunt thrashes his son with a hickory fork handle when he refuses to return to school.

Morton drifts into steady drinking and poker-playing with the crowd from town. Then he and the Gaunt family arrive at a truce which allows him to drop out of high school.

Morton had first met Marjie at a dance in Rutland. Matters are precipitated by his old grudge against Wes Allen, who is now

escorting Marjie. The story around the community was that
Marjie's dad had been once a fairly rich owner of a newspaper in
Brattleboro and had lost his position through drinking. Morton in
his jealous chivalry makes a *cause célèbre* out of separating
Marjie from Wes Allen. Marjie is interested mostly in getting
squired around Allenville and plays Wes Allen against Morton.
She succeeds for only a brief time but is told to change her living
habits or she must leave the home of her aunt and uncle. Morton
"rescues" Marjie by eloping and brings her to the Gaunt home.

The focus now turns to Sylvia. To acquaint us Brace gives a set
piece—a scene from her childhood that allows us to appreciate
her essentially poetic nature. She is described at eleven drifting
through a beautiful mid-May day, a kind of *Après-midi d'un
faune*. She is so lost in the glories of the Vermont hillside that she
fails to return home; she sleeps the night in the open apart from
her folks.

After graduation and observing Marjie's status in the Gaunt
family, Sylvia begins to wonder about her own future. Carrie
Gaunt shrewdly advises her to do nothing for a while but stay
home and help. Life asserts itself in the form of Lincoln McCann,
a thirty-eight-year-old English professor from Wyndham. He is
Henry's friend who hikes over the mountain for a visit. McCann's
simple honesty attracts Sylvia, who met him accidentally on the
hillside. McCann's volubility hides some rather sound ideas. He
defends his life. "All I want is a hundred students a year, and I
won't complain of the futility of college teaching. I admit that I
think some of my colleagues are fuddy duddies and that the
administration is just a branch of the First National Bank, but I
won't for that reason retire to a cabin in the mountains where I
can be alone with my virtue." When one stops to consider it, that
is not a bad working philosophy for the profession of college
teaching. One suspects that Brace himself might own up to a fair
share of agreement with this kind of thinking. Mr. Gaunt takes
exception to McCann's extolling of the wayward life, the desire
to simply sit under a tree and think. McCann pays much attention
to Sylvia.

Sylvia just before meeting McCann had turned down Tommy
Drew's offer of marriage. She cared for him but wanted some
more time before marriage and seemed to go deeper into her
dreams. Sylvia, Henry and the professor climb Stafford. Henry's
sprained ankle gives some privacy to McCann and Sylvia.

McCann's talk enchants Sylvia. Their moments on the mountain have drawn them close to each other. But there are hints from each that there are other commitments, "promises to keep."

After McCann returns with Henry to Wyndham, Sylvia's thoughts are not merely on McCann; she again luxuriates upon the Autumn mountainside rapturously. "All that mattered was the love itself, the chance to remember and to perceive, to live in the light of it, to know that life had possibility within it."

Sylvia does not lack admirers. John Scarci, a Catholic class-mate, an intelligent young son of a stonecutter, loves her. He's too much of a Democrat and an Italian for either John Gaunt or Morton to like. Scarci's valedictory address confirms old man Gaunt's views. Just another agitator. Sylvia has been serious about John Scarci, but her meeting with McCann brings a change. She patiently hears out Scarci's appeal for her to wait for him while he pursues an evening course in law in Boston. The rejection is, however, complete. The scene effectively closes with John realizing Sylvia's new feelings. But she remains for him like Shakespeare's Sylvia: "holy fair and wise is she."

On an October football weekend at Wyndham Sylvia stays with the McCanns and meets the professor's wife, Victoria Helen. Sylvia is struck by the difference between her beauty in a photograph on McCann's desktop and the impressions of the women herself. She is a woman who cares little for her husband and much for her bibelots, her social appearances, the grand dream of refinement that she shares with her British mother, Constance. When Sylvia returns from the dance she passes by McCann's study where the professor has spent the evening dreaming of her. McCann makes an open declaration of his love but tells her she need never do anything about his dreams. Hypnotized by the man in his university surroundings, Sylvia can think only of his loneliness.

They meet again at Thanksgiving at the Gaunts. On the mountain slope again McCann admires her beauty and asks hopefully if she has ever felt closer to the beauty of the mountains, as he softly kisses her. Sylvia responds: " 'Well, there have been lots of kinds, but not this kind. And if you hadn't come it would have been different.' He waited to hear more, but she shook her head impatiently. 'It's no good my trying to say anything.' " (p. 248)

In the closing section of the novel the reader is made aware of

Marjie's devastating effect on the Gaunt household. She had thought in her hasty marriage to Morton that somehow they would have an apartment in town. Now almost daily she seeks diversion by wandering back into town. Before Thanksgiving she speaks to Sylvia of leaving for good. Morton ignores her or treats her with brutality until he learns she is pregnant. The burden for her care falls chiefly on Carrie Gaunt, who has not taken to Marjie's wandering with a child on the way. Sylvia pitches in harder than ever and Carrie tries to allay Marjie's wild fears about delivery. Beverly Gaunt is born—much to Morton's disappointment. Carrie Gaunt suffers a stroke.

From this point on the Gaunt family fortunes markedly decline. Sylvia abandons McCann's offer of a scholarship. But she will not go on being the household drudge. Morton refuses even to go to town for groceries until Mr. Gaunt demands his cooperation. When Morton sees Henry trying to act humanly toward Marjie by giving her a ride to town, he accuses Henry of making advances. Morton forces a fight behind the barn with Henry, who avoids fighting until he is thrown to the ground. He then gives the out-of-shape Morton his comeuppance with a couple of clean blows.

When Mrs. Gaunt begins to make a slight recovery, Marjie shows some signs of an effort to help. Yet one afternoon, when she is alone with Mrs. Gaunt, Wes Allen drives in the yard and the baby is left behind with Mrs. Gaunt. Marjie returns to find the baby screaming and the stiff body of Mrs. Gaunt on the floor of the shed. She had probably died in her efforts to pacify the infant.

When Professor McCann talks with Sylvia just after the funeral of Mrs. Gaunt, he learns that Sylvia plans shortly to marry Tommy Drew. When Mr. Gaunt realizes that Sylvia will be no longer housekeeping with Henry off to graduate school, he reacts sharply. "Once you go, don't think you can come back—it'll be all over, all this. . . . It ain't that I want either of you gone, but I'm telling you how it is—how it will be. When the best of us go, and the worst stay, something bad's bound to come of it" (p. 317).

II   *A Novel in a New Vein*

Certainly, in contrast to *The Islands* and *The Wayward Pilgrims* Brace's *Light on a Mountain* contains a larger gallery of full-size portraits. Henry, Morton, Sylvia, Mr. and Mrs. Gaunt—all these lives are given full canvas. And one of the better qualities of the novel is the way the various crises of these people's lives are brought into focus. In the strictly technical sense the narrative point of view might be called omniscient. One could call Henry Gaunt the "good" hero, as Edward Wagenknecht points out,[2] but this designation seems to stretch the term out of its ordinary meaning. For Henry's goodness consists mainly of his little acts of kindness toward his family. He hardly dominates the action of the book. He is something like a Jamesian reflector, but not in the sense that Brace is using him as a central intelligence. Henry's values are identifiable with those the reader comes to associate generally with a Bracian hero: intelligence, manliness, love of the out-of-doors, and a sympathy for other people. The novel's most prominent theme, the impact on man of the beauty of the mountainous country, is conveyed most fully through the consciousness of Henry. But as the tale unfolds Henry's presence is felt through his absorption of experience from the lives of all the Gaunts, through his becoming a responsible human person in their drama.

Lincoln McCann at first appears to be a highly sympathetic figure, too. He is Henry's mentor and has the qualities one might expect to find in a more fully matured Henry. McCann is about twice Henry's age. But McCann's life has been thwarted by a marriage that has curtailed his potential. The McCanns are childless. The scene at their home convinces one that he and his wife live in the stultified air of cultural striving. The professor despite his joining in the hikes with Henry and Sylvia has retreated to ineffectual writing of books about books. McCann can still be sound in his criticism both of himself, the college and the changing times. He is honest in his desire to assist Sylvia's college career because he sees in her the same fine qualities that he finds in Henry. Thus we are made aware that the cultural values which are being probed in this novel have their roots in the kind of liberal education seen in the character of McCann. These liberal and intellectual crosscurrents flow through McCann to Henry, and through both McCann and Henry to Sylvia.

The McCann-Sylvia relationship is one of the most important in the story when we consider the central thematic tensions—the influence of the liberal-arts culture upon the life of the hill country family. Both Sylvia and Henry's fine sensibilities are faced with the harsh everyday reality of farm life in a declining economy. Sylvia's reactions to McCann are altogether credible. She had never known anyone such as he and is awed by his conversation and his refined manners. But while admitting to herself his attractiveness she intuits his marital situation and makes not the slightest move to further their love. McCann's pressure had begun to open up her mind, to put ideas in her head. She accedes to his idea of college for her. But when her mother dies and responsibility crowds in upon her life, she refuses her brother's request to talk further with McCann about college. "She shook her head slowly. No, that wouldn't do any good; he's got too many ideas." Has the transition been too sudden from poetic nymph to shrewd Vermont girl who correctly assesses that her best chances are with Tommy Drew? Is she simply too idealized a conception? Usually Brace anchors his characters in the actualities of everyday life. When she has to, Sylvia turns her hand very helpfully to others—to the business of living; the very last image in the novel is that of Sylvia going back into the house to show McCann and Henry how to change the baby's diaper and to remind Tommy Drew that it would be practical for him to learn, too. Sylvia is, in the final analysis, credibly drawn.

It is fair to say that the general tension between the intellectual life (as represented more by Henry Gaunt and Professor McCann) and the ordinary and difficult life of the farm is resolved neither in the favor of the former or of the latter. Henry Gaunt provides an aesthetic balance here. He is at home with saw or paint brush or behind the wheel of the truck, but he clearly also has his mind set on some larger accomplishments, too.

III   *Vermont Life*

The novel's portrayal of Vermont life is rich indeed. Good and honest and wholesome as the way of life of the Gaunts and their ancestors on Stratton Mountain had been, *Light on the Mountain* heralds, by focusing on a single dramatic year, the break-up of this tradition. This is effectively symbolized in the cutting down of the spruces at the beginning of the novel and in Henry's visit to the abandoned Martha Sargent cabin. The Sargent farm as a ghost of Vermont past reminds one of the images in such Frost poems as the early "Ghost House" (1913) and the much later "Directive" (1947).

In *Days That Were* Brace writes unabashedly about his love affair with Vermont. He recounts how as a young man starting out as a freshman at Amherst he regularly neglected his studies for the call of the neighboring hills. He pushed on into southern Vermont and, exhausted from a day's hiking and climbing, he encountered many remote farmhouses where farmers' hospitality (sometimes after a little hesitation) was extended to him. Some families, particularly the Hancocks and the Murdocks, became fast and lifelong friends of the novelist. These friends must have been transmuted into the Gaunts and the Carters of *The Wayward Pilgrims*. Particularly Brace speaks of his "natural affinity for the old-time New England female". He was searching for the past of New England as he imagined it. The following passage from *Days That Were* tells of the first of such ventures into the green mountains and articulates the vision underlying of *Light on a Mountain:*

But—there was Vermont at last, and I breathed its higher and pure air with relish. In the years to follow I was to see a great deal of it and for a while to feel almost native to it, and I remember my first entrance as though I had had a premonition of events to come. But I hardly expected the absolute beauty of its landscape, the mountains and high hills all arranged by a master designer, with rich green mowings in the valleys and golden pastures on the hills and dark forested mountain ranges folding away into the distances—and little clapboarded villages and white churches under elms and sugar maples and homesteads with great barns, and mowings and plowings and herds of placid cows. Not that I saw all such things in the dusk of that first evening, but every thing I did see from then on seemed to have a pristine Vermont quality about it. It all lay there like an immemorial Arcadia, except that it still displayed its old northern wilderness, with its mowings and pastures running up into the forests of spruce and fir on the mountain slopes. Even in the blossoming spring I felt the presence of the long winter somewhere in the offing.[3]

Light on a Mountain reflects much of the spirit of love of land as described in this excerpt. Brace admitted to (at that point in his young life) a "Currier and Ives" view of New England in general. Later, reflecting on the novel he suggested to an

Amherst audience that, in a critic's terms, the story might be called the end of his "early period." He also admitted that it was his "favorite" of all his stories and probably a better novel than the two previous. But chiefly he reaffirmed his great feeling of love for the hill country.[4]

It is necessary to realize that in writing of the breakup of the Gaunt family Brace is not permitting his sentiments about Vermont to interfere with his assessment of human existence in a New England of the late 1930s. The old ways were decent good ways, but a significant change is seen in Sylvia's fiancé's interest in electronics. Tommy Drew and Sylvia will open a radio agency in town.

The future of Morton Gaunt, on the other hand, is indeed a dark one. Marjie is again pregnant and he is without any sympathy for her human needs. In front of McCann and the family Morton literally handles her as if she were so much horseflesh. He retains all the energy and ingenuity that his forebears had in their struggles with the land. But unfortunately he doesn't possess the intelligence needed to adapt in a changing world. Nor does there seem to be any resource from which he could acquire a modicum of human decency, some regard for rights and feelings of other humans on the planet. Marjie is even less equipped for survival. We sense that she is incapable of living without the help of stronger minds and bodies to assist her, and these do not appear. Something like Joan Lathrop of *The Islands*, she is not much fitted for struggle in the modern world. As we shall see Brace continued to view New England as a microcosm. If his novels appear to be quite in a different mode from leading realists of the period, one feels that partly the reason is that his love of his adopted land of New England leads him into a somewhat romantic handling of the New England life in his fiction. If this is true, for example, in the characterizations of Henry Gaunt and his sister, it is also true to say that Brace never shrank from the ugly aspects of the same New England character as witnessed in the behavior of Henry's brother. As a further example of this sort of realistic perception we have the tendency throughout his novels to depict usually one character fully in the novel who comes to despair and/or suicide.

A decade later in the novel *The Spire* the author in a kind of Trollopian economy of creation took up the career of Henry

Gaunt after college and, to a lesser degree, the career of his sister Sylvia.

CHAPTER 4

"Success"

T HE mention of Gerald Warner Brace's name to those who are
somewhat familiar with the American novel of the twentieth
century is apt to bring to mind *The Garretson Chronicle.* The
book became a best seller in 1947 and is easily Brace's most
popular fiction. It is a realistic chronicle told in the first person as
a memoir by Ralph Garretson, who in his forties is assessing his
past life experience. He renders through the use of dramatic
episodes the life of three generations of the Garretson family,
who lived in the small town of Compton, Massachusetts, not far
from Concord (the famous center of New England Transcendentalism). Ralph's grandfather Theodore is but one generation
removed from the famous figures of Concord itself and the
action of the story moves forward to the mid 1940s. To bring off
successfully such a novel largely through the use of an
intellectual irony which renders a basic criticism of the Compton
way of life is a difficult thing to achieve. But Brace does just this
with great finesse, using his manifest verbal craftsmanship, his
knowledge of architectural design, and his maturing insights into
homo sapiens, species Yankee.

To begin with, Ralph Garretson has a fine critical sensitivity
and an ironical turn to go with it. If being a rebel is an
indigenously American and especially Yankee quality, then
Ralph's credentials are well founded to start with. He found
himself dropped from Harvard at the end of his second year in
1920, as a result of his "motiveless rebellion." He did not
associate, however, with the "lost generation" group of artists
and social dissenters. We might conceive that his rebellious
nature could have shaped itself around that of those political and
aesthetic rebels of the 1920s and 1930s; but his individualism is
better understood as rooted rather in the New England past. He
might have stayed on at Harvard and followed the regimen of

courses, but his individualism would not permit him to do this. "My defections grew out of idlement and uncertainty." Ralph's chronicle is important because it provides the reader with an intelligent account of how an honest person came to terms with himself, with a world in ferment and with his New England past, which the Garretsons represent so characteristically.

When he sets down his memoir Ralph is forty-four. We can assess the character of the writer in Ralph as one who always had the desire to write even though, as matters turned out, writing did not become his main profession. His episodic chronicle of events is carefully written. The reader's interests throughout are caught up in the flow of life from one generation to the next, because of Ralph Garretson's own sustaining interest in these people, as people.

What gives *The Garretson Chronicle* its fine integrity as a first-person narrative is the manner in which the author's attitudes or ironies toward his material become merged with Ralph Garretson's ironies and attitudes. The heaviness and/or sharpness of these ironies tend to diminish as Ralph Garretson himself matures with life. At forty-four, he has become largely what he is from the inevitable influences that earlier have shaped his life, but, at the same time, he has clearly mellowed with the passage of time. He has come to understand and to counter the crosscurrents of his existence in New England. Critics of the book have not stressed enough the subtlety into which Brace's attitude toward his subject mixes with that of his narrator. True, this kind of mixing tends sometimes toward the inextricable or the ambiguous as it does, say, in Henry James. But the game is worth the candle.

Near the beginning of the chronicle Ralph observes that most of the men of his college generation got only a little way toward their supposed abandonment of belief. "It was said to be a result of war, that lostness; but it always came from more than war, more than a few young men reveling in disillusion. . . . We advanced from faith into reason, and so in time we shall come round to faith again" [1] (p. 6). What is uttered here by Ralph Garretson is consonant with the kind of person he develops into as the novel progresses. The kind of truth Garretson here registers has not been said often in American fiction of the period that *The Garretson Chronicle* belongs to.

I *Theodore Garretson*

Grandfather Theodore Garretson is the focus of the first three chapters of the book. Ralph composes the portrait from his own reminiscenses of life in the ancestral home and from the public image his grandfather made as a first citizen of Compton and from the novels and essays that Theodore had written. He had started out as a Congregational minister and had left that occupation when his didactic novels offered him a better livelihood. He had moved to Compton probably to be near the literary center of Concord. His was the Emersonian life of plain living and high thinking. Yet he could not really afford the colonial house that he purchased and which later became one of the treasures of the town. His novels became the moral tracts, common for those times, aimed against drink and other pleasures. Man's abstinence in these pursuits supposedly brought a better chance for money and social position. At eighty, Theodore had not produced any books for several years; but the old man continued to write at his desk for a few hours each morning, and periodically send out letters to the *Boston Transcript*.

Ralph was "brought up in a tradition of liberality and democracy, and actually in an atmosphere of class distinction." The grandfather belonged to a circle of minor notables including Charles Edward Mayo, the poet to whom God and Nature were one. "It seems the old boy was spiritually akin to Dante, and in the end succeeded in resolving the tragic duality of American matter and spirit—contrasting in this respect with the notable failure of Melville and Whitman." Mayo wrote poems on haymaking and died at seventy-two by working too hard with a scythe (this walloping irony speaks much for itself and for Ralph as well). Another holdover in the village from the heyday of Transcendentalism is Franklin Gray, the ornithologist of the town who claims to have never done a day's work in his life; the village boys always trailed along behind him. It should be affirmed, however, that these people did the thing they loved best.

The best friends of Ralph were the Madigans, who lived in the poorer section of town near the factories. Their father drove Theodore's carriage. It is abundantly clear that Ralph's basic education came about via fighting, fishing, ball playing, and the other such liberal arts of juvenile life; these studies were the direct result of contact with the Madigans, especially Tom, the eldest. Grandfather Garretson would have robbed Ralph's life of its true poetic beginnings. There was the instance of the organ grinder who would not stop playing "The Wearing of the Green" outside the Garretson residence. Ralph was charged by Theodore to call the police until Lucy Garretson, Ralph's stepmother, paid the customary amount and the grinder moved along.

The psychological climax for Ralph in those early years at the Garretson home came when Tom Madigan, the natural leader of the group, conceived the idea of a tree house to be built from lumber and materials from the Garretson barn and then mounted on the maples in the front yard with a pulley to hoist up the necessary items. Theodore Garretson appears and the boys are respectful of his commands to desist, but the tone of the grandfather's remark that "I will not allow boys of this sort to play here" is a chilling and wounding one for his eleven-year-old grandson. To clinch the insult Theodore Garretson later calmly affirms his underlying feelings: "Riffraff and micky boys . . . I simply had to draw the line."

II   Randall Garretson

The second main section of the book centers on the life of Ralph's father, Randall. Novelist Brace through these chapters has his narrator make use of his father's journals to aid his own memory in the reconstruction of the career of a "man who felt himself a worthy disciple of the great."

Randall was the third child of four and got Theodore's special attention after the fourth child had died. He went to grade school in Compton but got instruction in Latin, Greek, and Christianity from Theodore. By sixteen he had read all of Plato and was ready for Harvard. He confessed long afterwards that he had never bothered with Plato again. Later his journal began to show the advent of influence from another sphere: Ruskin, Morris, Swinburne, and Pater. He told Ralph that "everything we lived for could be put into one word: beauty, only beauty. The pure gemlike flame." When Ralph was flirting with communism Randall was watching to "see how much of an ass I made of myself. 'But you don't get so much fun out of it, Ralph. Even your follies are grim.'" Randall himself dreams of a career such as James Russell Lowell's or Charles Elliot Norton's and reads Keats, Sappho, Virgil, and especially Thoreau.

When their mother dies Theodore takes Randall and his sister, Jean, on a European tour. Randall falls in love with Eileen Warrener. His dreams of womanly loveliness fade in the light of this "cool little mistress of life and manners" as they pay their homage to all the masterworks in Europe. In Rome together they read again *Daisy Miller* and the *Marble Faun* and in front of the Basilica of St. Peter, Randall proposes. But Eileen Warrener has really no interest. Randall comes back to Compton and begins architecture school, in Boston, feeling that this profession "turns art to profit and cultivates a sensitive taste with practical results." A summary, from Ralph's perspective, of his father, merits quotation:

He learned how to reproduce the classic orders and to draw the elevations of Gothic vaulting. He was instructed in imitations. Architects in that time were humble men, as I understand it; they looked upon the three great periods of the past much as a common wayfarer might look at the peaks of the Himalayas. There on equal terms with the heaven itself, stood the pure and shining classic, the Parthenon indistinguishable from celestial snows; and there, too, the aspiring Gothic, the fartherest heavenward shaft ever shot by man; and there the domed Italian, man's own pomp and pride somehow equated with God's. In the shadow of such grandeur, the modern man on earth could do no other than worship. He made a phrase of it—The Great Tradition—and appointed himself as keeper; he established the orders and preserved the codes. He imitated not in ignorance but in patient wisdom and learned respect. His memorial halls and libraries expressed only one faith: that the past was forever glorious and the present was contemptible. The mountain peaks were for other men in other times; here we lived in the valley and the shadow, looking always back and up. (pp. 67-68)

When Eileen Warrener marries an Englishman, it takes some time for Randall to get over it. He becomes friends of the Hollisters on Marlborough Street in Back Bay, wealthy Bostonians who summered in Maine and in the White Mountains. Mrs. Hollister was from the Bradstreet line. Of her three daughters, Alice, the oldest, seemed most likely to carry on the Bradstreet traditions. Mr. Hollister had died leaving a large annual income from house rents in South Boston. Randall "admired" Alice, "loved May as a sister," and "truly loved" Caroline, the young and pure, who was somewhat self-conscious about her buxomness and yet the envy of her sisters. Alice, who had worked at the Settlement House and who read Bellamy's *Looking Backward,* deftly turns Randall's attentions away from Caroline and walks down the aisle with him after a year.

The largest crisis in Randall's life comes early in his marriage. Alice is pulled toward the city, the Copley Forum, and the Lowell Lectures. She can't see the practicality of all of Randall's talk about what Compton means to him with his writing of odes to its seasons and landscape and old houses. For him, civilization clearly is not of the city; its essence was somehow in Compton. Even the summer trips to Mt. Desert are not his idea of true pleasure. When they return from Maine not long after their marriage, the head of the architectural firm advises Randall that his talents are no longer really suitable for the steel construction that is becoming the vogue. The impact on the dreamy Randall is muted. He will return to Compton to live and there will be a greater opportunity for his writing. He will make the world see Compton in all its artistic glories.

Alice Hollister is horrified at Randall's drifting, and at the living at the Garretson home, but she tries this life for a time. There are now three young Garretsons and Randall's prospects are no more definite. Eventually Alice's health deteriorates. The doctor warns that an entirely different atmosphere, a change of scene is vital for her. Alice demands to be removed from the Garretson home and finally proposes that they all go to California for a new start. But the bond between them is severed after a divorce. Alice leaves Compton and the three children remain with their father. When Theodore is dying he calls young Ralph to his bedside; he sees in him the bearer one day of the Garretson aegis; he stresses "that the conditions of peace and freedom and moral good exist only because a few people strive to maintain them." Ralph is impressed by the tone even if the thoughts are not very clear.

III *Ralph*

The third section of the book is Ralph's own story. His father remarries; Lucy Brattle is a Compton girl, with important family

ties; she is a Smith College graduate, a devoted botanist, a
Unitarian, and an intellectual. Lucy is highly efficient, but love is
missing in their union. Ralph becomes the family misfit. He is
large-framed and clumsy in his teens. Unlike his friends the
Madigans, he attends the Bronson Alcott School, founded by the
Channings. In a major episode, the dancing instructor assigns
Ralph to the tallest girl. "Beanpole" begins to cry and his
attempts to comfort her are gallant enough but Christina's grief
is beyond his help.

The major influences in Ralph's life develop out of a chance
visit to the Kingsley's farm a short distance outside of Compton.
When his mother sends him for eggs, he has difficulty
approaching the place because of their dogs; but Mrs. Kingsley is
watching from the window and tells him "to come in and do the
talking after."

The whole way of life of the Kingsleys enchants Ralph: their
Eden-like land, Seth Kingsley's craftsmanship as a cabinet
maker; his way of making maple sugar; young Martha Kingsley's
warmth. Seth gradually becomes Ralph's mentor. He has respect
for the Garretsons. He sounds out Ralph on his ambitions and
curbs Ralph's prejudices with a sharp Yankee understatement:
"Once you acknowledge truth to yourself . . . then you're stuck
with it. Anything less won't work." His family reluctantly let
Ralph hire out summers to work for the Kingsleys. He learns how
to swing a scythe and stack a load of hay. He loves Martha, who
works with him with an "almost mystic devotion."

Ralph's idyll with the Kingsleys is interrupted by his entering
Lincoln Prep School, a New England Rugby with its caste system
of graduated football squads that are supposed to build
leadership. When he is disciplined, he is daring enough to
confront the headmaster with a question of his own about the
disappearance of Thoreau and Emerson. The headmaster
responds: "Your Thoreau and Emerson . . . were brilliant
individualists and observers; they took no part in the great
practical labors of mankind—in fact, like so many men of genius,
they evaded much of their manifest destiny" (p. 227). Ironically
Ralph's real education is going on in Seth Kingsley's woodworking shop, whenever he can manage the opportunity. There he
comes to terms with mahogany and steel and precise measure-
ments. He learns the satisfaction of fine craftsmanship, of a piece
of furniture made durably and beautifully by the hands.

In his senior year at Lincoln, Ralph affects a cynicism about the world's problems. The United States entered the war in April, but he is slightly underage for service beyond the ROTC drills at the school. He goes to Harvard for two years, only to be dropped for lack of any real effort. While there he is not allied with either of the two principal factions on campus: the old, fashionable, exclusive set obsessed with social distinctions or the more voluble and demonstrative moderns who do not share any belief in the old Harvard or *any* Harvard, for that matter. These latter are wallowing in their disillusionment and Ralph drifts without any real joy or commitment to their side. They publish "The Devil's Advocate," but they are not yet riding a very popular tide. D. H. Lawrence and Sherwood Anderson and Dos Passos are just beginning to find readers. Ralph in retrospect feels, however, that Harvard fulfills the real function of a university. It is like a Great Bank. "It both stores and issues knowledge. . . . Not any human weal or woe officially concerns it—nothing but the knowledge it holds and increases and issues with incorruptible integrity." But he cautions his readers that even Harvard's "worship of knowledge, about life itself" may have been a part of America's sense of material values.

IV   The Women in His Life

Like his father and his grandfather, too, Ralph has a desire to write. Seth Kingsley sees in Ralph's departure from Harvard an important fork of the road. He is reluctant to see the loss of educational opportunity that takes Ralph out of the orbit of the leadership in the community. Randall Garretson still knows more of the architectural styles of old Compton than any man alive. Ralph continues to work irregularly with Seth, who is himself fighting a battle with cheaper mass-produced furniture. Seth prefers to hire himself out as a carpenter, causing Ralph to take a job in Waltham in a factory that produces ironing-boards and clothes-reels. At night he reads the Russian novelists, a door that Harvard had not opened for him. Ralph feels that this Waltham business is mainly Babbittry, although he gets along well with Mr. Quinn, who is in failing health and has an eye on Ralph to take over his business. Mr. Quinn lives with an invalided wife and with his daughter Marilyn, who shares Ralph's first serious love. At first Marilyn looks down upon Ralph as another workman until

she learns about his Lincoln schooling. Up to this point Martha
Kingsley has been Ralph's dream girl, his "pioneer bride,"
without her ever knowing it. Martha had gone to Pennsylvania to
become a nurse and Ralph had learned how later she had gone to
Florida hoping to be married there and had been deserted. As
for Marilyn "I lived," says Ralph, "that absurd and secret and
terrible life of desire all men live. . . . Yet no record embodies
that life. Some quality of taste, old habit, cowardice kept me
from experience. . . . So my passions remained suppressed and
secret."

Mr. Quinn detests the social set that Marilyn has been aspiring
to and Ralph has been looking around to find his dream girl in
Boston's Marlborough Street set. But on the sofa at the Quinn's
he and Marilyn are becoming intimate. Mr. Quinn has hoped for
such an outcome and urges Ralph to marry his daughter, after
the two have already drifted into an agreement to marry.
Marilyn, however, likes to attend the country club dances; and
though Ralph indulges her, he dislikes this life intensely. One
evening he finds himself momentarily alone at the dance.
Marilyn has gone off to enjoy a brief lark with some of her crowd.
He speaks with a woman who like himself seems lost. In the
darkness of the dance hall the two exchange their thoughts and
find a bond of intellectual sympathy. When the woman asks him
to dance Ralph remembers: she is Christina or "Beanpole," his
boyhood dancing partner. It is an effective scene as Ralph begins
to realize that the girl whose adolescent physical traits had been
the object of his boyish scorn, now has a manner and appearance
full of grace and charm.

At twenty-two, Ralph is chafed more and more by the social
constraints that Marilyn brings—the wedding preparations and
the obligations that loom ahead, including the managing of a
business. He fears that the grimness of Mr. Quinn's way of life
will become his. But most of all, without his realizing it, the
image of "Beanpole" is beginning to permeate his being.

Two Harvard friends go with Ralph on an October weekend
climb to Mt. Washington. Although the weather is not favorable,
they drive to Pinkham Notch in Ralph's old Ford. As they climb,
ice appears in the woods and on the north side of the mountain.
They persist in the climb and lose their bearings in a great wind
storm. Separately they try to work their way down the mountain.
In the morning, one of the three is found dead. Ralph ends up in a

hospital in New Hampshire. Randall comes to the hospital and the two have a kind of reconciliation. His father's talk seems no longer to have its accustomed edge of irony. He speaks of New England as a microcosm: it had its own middle ages; its renaissance, and its reformation. In this view old Theodore Garretson represented the theocratic aspect; the Harvard scholars had brought the new classic age with its religious liberalism, its new art and literature; then industrialism had come upon them. In Compton one could find all of these historic kinds living together. When Ralph asks what age his father represented, Randall refers to himself as an anachronism, representing all but the present. His counsel to Ralph is to look ahead regardless of the prospects.

Ralph's own thoughts were intensified by the mountain experience:

I saw the mountain continually, not as a special and temporary experience, but as the very arrowhead of reality, the lethal head of Nature itself, sort of an inlander's Moby Dick, white as all eternity and beautiful as heavenly truth and far beyond good and evil—beyond any range of mortal value; and I felt inclined to worship that power not in love and hope, but simply in recognition of it as the inescapable weapon of destiny. Mine was no Ahab spirit, to hurl myself singlehanded against infinity; I had no desire to tilt with cosmic windmills; I accepted the mountain, humbly and with awe, as the sort of fact that my limited will had to make the best of. Just then I had no fight left in me, though I've since realized that the will is by nature a fighter and sallies forth again and again to test the immortal enemy: Ahab and Quixote must be the brackets in which all men are enclosed. (p. 324)

V   A Change of Life

After recuperating at the Garretson home for awhile, Ralph concocts a plan to head west in his Ford with one of the Madigan brothers. Terry Madigan accepts the idea. When he visits the Kingsleys he is reminded by them that he has been shunting off, since the mountain tragedy, his engagement and Marilyn's final preparations for the marriage. Ralph drives to Waltham and blurts out his inner feelings—his wish to cancel the engagement. Marilyn's only feeling is that Ralph's friend's death has caused it all. Mr. Quinn blames the situation on Ralph's upbringing—nice manners and games rather than real obligations to be met. Ralph is glad to let it rest at that and heads west, realizing more and more what the depths of his feelings toward Christina Ross were.

After a year of roughing it, Ralph returns to a warm reception from Christina, but not from her widow mother, an independent Scotswoman who lives above the pharmacy she owns. She is very cool toward Ralph's desire for marriage. She would much rather return to Scotland and make a match there for her daughter than to allow her to remain in America and marry shiftless Ralph Garretson. When Ralph proposes, Christina questions him about his future and learns of his philosophy of living life on its own terms—"in terms of its own materials." Ralph would follow Stein's advice in Conrad's *Lord Jim.* He would acquire strength from the very destructive element itself. Christina will make no commitment. Ralph returns to work with Seth Kingsley, designing and making furniture and doing some writing—becoming a village carpenter in his father's view. Mrs. Ross and Christina depart for Scotland for an indefinite stay.

When Seth Kingsley is injured in a fall from a roof, Ralph moves in with the family and assumes Seth's work. His final commitment is to craftsmanship in his native Compton. When the Rosses return, Mrs. Ross provides some difficult moments, but it is clear that Christina wants Ralph. There is a reconciliation of sorts with his father, too. When a buyer of one of the old houses in Compton wishes to restore the place, Seth recommends Randall Garretson as the only man who can act as consultant. The house symbolizes the tension between the visions of father and son. Randall calls Ralph's reality flesh and blood, hammer and nails; Ralph continues to see his father's reality as vision itself. As the two approach the Garretson home, Randall tells Ralph of his desire to give him his patrimony now, when it can aid him in marrying. Brace closes the novel with a vignette of Ralph's modest success over the succeeding years in working with Mr. Kingsley, of Christina's unselfish support; of their modest farm home and children, not far from the valley where the Kingsleys live in view of the Compton elms and maples.

The *Garretson Chronicle* is the longest work of Gerald Warner Brace and a good case can be made for it as being the best book that he had written or would ever write. It is richly done. Its prose cadences are finely fashioned like the furniture that comes from Seth Kingsley's workshop—highly finished and polished. It is a style that sustains the prolonged intellectual probing of Ralph Garretson's mind and conveys to the reader Ralph's love of the material universe as well; Brace is never far from *le mot juste* that is needed to express the situation. And the novelist's practiced ear seldom fails to come up with the concrete term or the turn of phrase that carries conviction in the dialogue sequences. Many first-person narratives of extended length fail to be completely convincing along these lines. *The Garretson Chronicle* rewards the reader continuously, even upon multiple readings.

Edward Wagenknecht, a fellow teacher of English with Gerald Brace at Boston University when this novel was written, wrote an assessment of the first five Brace novels (including *A Summer's Tale*, 1951), and was genuinely sympathetic about his achievements. He especially admired *The Garretson Chronicle*, yet he felt "for a time we even lose the boy who is supposed to be telling the story."[2] One supposes that Wagenknecht is here referring to the chapters that deal with the breakup of the marriage of Alice Hollister and Randall Garretson, which occurred when Ralph was about nine. But it is not quite accurate to insist here on a "boyish" narrator because it is clear that we are following the recreation of an older man using his father's journals to that purpose. During this section of the novel the narrator does not make much commentary on the parent's life, but there is good dramatic use of the scenes as developed by Ralph's imagination from the journals. To lose the narrator's voice under such controlled circumstances may be an artistic effect that is intended rather than not.

If we broaden the question of this aspect of the novel and consider the general looseness or episodic structure of the story or chronicle in relation to the narrative voice, it becomes clear that there is a successful blending of the two selves: the younger experiencing self and the older retrospective self combine during the course of the story, harmonize, and return to each other as the novel closes. The risk the writer takes in attempting to achieve this reunion in an episodic structure must be ever present to him and probably tends toward his creating an intrusive or labored effect. But Brace's selectivity of scene and maintenance of dramatic tensions work well, in my estimation, to achieve good flow and good narrative pace. When Ralph's later life assumes major focus in the story, one feels no sense of interruptedness.

In a well-known essay on the American novel written in 1940 shortly before Brace's novel, Philip Rahv downgraded American novelists with the exception of Henry James for their inability to create characters with significant intellectual dimensions.[3] Twain, Hemingway, Dos Passos, Steinbeck and others are seen as militating against true cerebration in their writing. Ralph Garretson, of course, is using retrospection in his review of his past life from his boyhood to his early full maturity. But Brace does successfully exhibit a quality of thinking in his major character. Ralph thinks about his cultural environment and thinks about it in a critical fashion. At the same time the hero is of native American stamp in his rebelliousness, in his love of work and in his love of the out-of-doors. Edgar Thurlow in *The Islands* was more of the craftsman and less of the thinker. Lawrence Minot of *The Wayward Pilgrims* and Henry Gaunt of *Light on the Mountain* approached more the quality of mind of Ralph Garretson. But Ralph's articulateness alone and his honesty of mind make him deserving of the term "intellectual" and yet this quality is subordinated and kept in balance by the love of the artisan for his work. The sharpest emotional moments of the book are those when Ralph is with Seth Kingsley and his wood-working tools, lost in his love of the mastery of the craft and the very smells of the shop. Ralph's dual concern (head in solitude and hand in society) might appear, after all, to be but another variation of the transcendentalism of his forbears. Yet there are many differences of importance to be recognized.

VI   *A Criticism of the Heritage*

In the portraits of Theodore and Randall Garretson as we receive them from Ralph, there is heavy emphasis on their divorcement from people, especially those of a lower status in Compton. Both Alice Hollister and Lucy Brattle are also least admirable in their tendencies to snobbery. Is Ralph himself altogether and convincingly free from this inheritance? Ralph gravitates toward the Madigans consistently both early and later in his life because he feels simply that there is more life to be lived with them. When he turns from Marilyn Quinn and begins to court Christina, it does not appear to be out of dislike for her and the Quinns in their social situation; it is more that Marilyn is becoming too acquisitive in her search for status: whereas

Christina is like Ralph, willing to meet people on their own terms; she likes to think things through.

C. Hugh Holman praises Brace highly for maintaining the "cultural propriety" of the narrator's dramatic voice:

It would be impossible to exaggerate the contribution which Brace's style makes to the accomplishment of the complex objectives which he sets for himself in *The Garretson Chronicle*. Ralph Garretson speaks always with dramatic and cultural propriety in that the mask never fails or falls, even when he withdraws from the action and reconstructs it, as he does in the sections of his father's early life, or when he abandons action for commentary. He always has cultural propriety in that he never violates the concept of the attitudes of his class, even while he is in rebellion against them. Ralph is created for us by the polished consistency of his style, and he, in turn, creates the surrounding world through his impressions of it. Everything—grace of movement, balance, choice of work, the highly intellectualized nature of his imagery, much of it borrowed from a wide range of writers, and the careful but lively shape of the sentences themselves—contributes to making Ralph a credible character and yet a thoroughly recognizable representative of his class and culture.[4]

What Holman describes above is very much in the Jamesian tradition of the novel, the immediacy of felt experience or life. However, it appears to me that what gives special dramatic tension to this novel is precisely Ralph's substantial disagreement with his cultural inheritance. In a similar context Holman speaks of how Brace is attracted to the concept of moderation which is linked to the eighteenth century as the Age of Reason: "Certainly he [Brace] has taken ambivalent attitudes toward the characters whose choices between 'the social necessities and the individual rights' are the dramatic heart of his work." The critic is here generalizing about the characteristics of all Brace's novels, but I do not feel that this view is accurate about the values that Ralph Garretson achieves in the book. Ralph, while keeping the essential manners and the bearing of his New England family inheritance, has steered quite steadily a course towards an acceptance of the ordinary world of ordinary people, after he has made the break from his family at the end of his sophomore year at Harvard. Brace's achievement, which is a considerable one, has not been only that for which Holman commends him—consistency in the dramatic voice; there is also a remarkable moral commitment and moral change that has been effected in the character of Ralph Garretson. Ralph desires to fulfill his social life in a way that is vastly different from that of his father. It appears, at the end of the story, that Ralph's ideas and his decisions with their clear emphasis on individual human honesty have been fruitful, far more so than have those of the rest of the Garretsons. Ralph's closing remarks are very modest: "My discoveries in life are here for whatever they are worth— and the worth may seem slight in an age of power. Alone, one is a small thing and the simple life seems out of place, just as air and earth and fire and water are out of place among the elements." Over against these words are those of Ralph's father as he sits with the grandchildren, lifting Ralph's axe and feeling its edge and handle. "I suppose I'm a little too old to learn to use it. If there were time, you could teach me a good deal, Ralph."

These last words of the text of the novel draw our attention to the achieved happiness of Ralph Garretson, and the words are free of the irony one finds in earlier parts of the story. The direction that Ralph's life is assuming is neither an ambivalent nor a socially anticonventional direction. Nor is it true that Brace is pointing to Ralph's solution as a code to follow. Ralph is contributing in a modest fashion to the community in which he expects to live out his life. This successful ending strikes the reader as significantly different from the majority of novels which deal with the lives of post-World War I heroes and their disillusionments of various kinds. The axe image previously referred to at the novel's end may be paired with that of a jack-knife which Ralph gives to Christina as a present just before her trip to Scotland. It appears to be an odd sort of present to give, but it signifies all that Ralph hopes for—the kind of life he could eventually share with her as an artisan at Seth Kingsley's shop. Christina in the early days of their marriage works by his side, caring for the tools. Her acts are emphasized. She has an "intense Scotch realism, with an austerity matching the place itself, with the fierce energy of a born artist." The accent at the ending of *The Garretson Chronicle* is reminiscent also of the closing section of *The Islands.* In that situation the heroine, Isabel Allen, picks up Edgar Thurlow's chisel and cuts her hand on its very fine edge. The novelist seems at this point to be preparing the reader for the separation of the pair by indicating that Edgar's life experience has honed his being in such a fine way as to be improperly matched with that of the inexperienced Isabel. Ralph Garretson's life may not be very heroic or very representative but it certainly does, in the Frostian sense, give us a momentary stay against the confusion of the twentieth century.

VII   *Cather and Marquand*

In some respects Brace may be compared with another novelist of the earlier twentieth century, Willa Cather, with whom he has a fair amount of sympathy. Readers will recall her prefatory thoughts in *Not Under Forty* about the world breaking in two somewhere around 1922.[5] For many years Cather critics interpreted her views on values as presented in this book to be a signaling of her divorce from essential social issues and they claimed her later novels accentuated this tendency in that she sought her heroes and her milieu from the "lovely past." To a considerable extent critics such as Maxwell Geismar chose to equate Cather's interest in this "lovely past" with what they felt was a concept of *laudator temporis acti* which seemed to imply a degeneration of present values. But to choose one's values in the past is not necessarily to make a fossil of oneself or one's concept of human values. Some of Willa Cather's most memorable moments convey the concept of timelessness rather than a celebration of a historical point in time. One recalls her celebration of the artifacts of the Pueblo civilization uncovered by Tom Outland in *The Professor's House* and his vain effort to interest the officials in the nation's capital in the preservation of Indian artifacts. In *My Ántonia* the ploughshare caught against the setting sun upon the prairie's distant horizon speaks to the young high-school graduates of the necessity of each generation of pioneers to labor on the land.

There is another aspect to this question. It is interesting to note that both Brace and Willa Cather had formal educational backgrounds with firm grounding in the classical languages and mores. It is neither surprising nor wrongheaded in either of them to create characters like Jim Burden and Ralph Garretson who want to retain something from the values of their forbears as well as a desire to probe honestly into the current life around them and to adversely criticize it.

In *The Garretson Chronicle* Ralph is coming to his majority at precisely that point which Willa Cather reckoned was so critical in our cultural history. Throughout his chronicle Ralph returns periodically to the Kingsley farm as the locus of his values. In Martha Kingsley there is something of the spirit that Jim Burden found so abundantly in the Bohemian girl Ántonia. What Jim Burden realizes at the end of the Cather novel is that the essence of life was somehow bound up with the sod hut existence of the Shimerdas and later the farm life on the prairie. Similarly, New England mores of the middle class are represented by the Kingsleys' existence in *The Garretson Chronicle*. Their small farm produced for themselves and for others. The endless "chores" of the farm were divided among all the family members. When Ralph joins them in an "adopted" fashion he begins to assume a fair share of the multiple duties of the place. It is interesting to note that Seth Kingsley's woodworking shop where he turns out his pure or classically styled furniture is located on the farm itself and hence integrated with the total operation. Thus Ralph experiences from the Kingsleys a holistic approach to life that had not been his fortune to have with the Garretsons in Compton itself. Brace is drawing here upon an authentic side of New England tradition of the smaller towns and areas. (I remember my own grandfather who ran a ten-acre small farm on the outskirts of town in Calais, Maine; he had a "marble shop" in one corner of the land from which he carried on his principal business of letter-engraving on tombstones. He budgeted part of his day in the shop and the rest on working the farm.)

Ralph Garretson says about his living with the Kingsleys: "I took things without earning them—Mrs. Kingsley's heart, Seth's mastery of materials, many things." Even though Ralph finally helps Seth to put power tools in the shop, it does not mean that either of them are chucking tradition. They are combining the best of their tradition as they see it with the most useful technological advances and their methods meet with fair success when their reputation for fine work gets around. Ralph's adaptability helps his family through the Depression. Seth Kingsley's values are not overtly Christian, but he does counsel Ralph that he might "find out a few things" by attending church services. Christina Ross's first name may be a further suggestion that Christian values are not incompatible but instead, consonant with the values that Ralph Garretson found life exhibits.

Another general comparison may be drawn between some of

the work of John P. Marquand and Gerald W. Brace in order to give a perspective on Brace's fiction. These two writers came from roughly similar social backgrounds, were familiar with the Harvard scene, and were exact contemporaries. It is profitable, I believe, to make a general comparison of the tone of their work and their attitudes toward New England life in the modern world. As a satirist Marquand kept steadily in focus the upper middle classes. The familiar plot of his novels followed the middle-aged hero's struggle to maintain his equilibrium in the business, social, or artistic world. Critic Charles A. Brady has written a delightfully lucid essay on Marquand's habitual backtracking into the past of his protagonists. He claims it is reflective of the author's own "psychological plight" that Marquand cannot forget the road not taken. Charles Brady is probably the only critic willing to do Marquand full justice by calling him "closer to the central novel than any writer of our period" (the early twentieth century). Some of Brady's further points about Marquand are: that he is a born satirist in the Horatian vein; that he was snubbed at Harvard; that both patrician and commoner blood were mixed in him. He further states that "as for Mr. Marquand and Mr. Marquand's readers, God can be felt in His absence as well as in His presence. This consciousness, keen to the point almost of being a sense of deprivation, constitutes a real spiritual dimension. God is by no means absent from the sad temporality of Marquand's novels."[6]

Both *The Garretson Chronicle* and *The Late George Apley* are highly successful in giving the reader full portraits of exemplars of a dying culture. Marquand is, however, essentially a very sharp and at the same time very urbane satirist. Satire in Brace's novel is very much more muted; it is concealed in lighter irony and it ultimately reflects a more sympathetic view of the New England past. Marquand's novels by and large treat of the New England middleaged hero facing the question of acceptance of the path of life he has chosen, his marriage and his fortunes. Marquand wrote primarily of the middle-class society that essentially he came from; he was a grandnephew of Margaret Fuller, the feminist champion, and he was related through marriage to Edward Everett Hale, the Boston Unitarian preacher and writer. It was natural for him to see his characters emerging into a newer society against the backdrop of this old one. Marquand's town of Clyde becomes a focus for old values in

perspective but most of the time his characters move in the
martini cocktail environment of a modern business world.

Brace's forebears were about as illustrious as Marquand's. But
they were not closely associated with Boston society. It should be
basically understood that Brace adopted New England as in a
sense did Robert Frost and a good many other writers, including,
in her last years, Willa Cather. And he adopted all of it. That is
he came to know best and love best the Maine coast where he
summered all of his life from childhood on. *The Islands* testifies
to his thorough intimacy with its land and its people. But Brace
also loved the mountains, especially those of Vermont, and the
folks that he found there working out their existences as best
they knew how, as is seen in *The Wayward Pilgrim* and more
especially in *Light on a Mountain*. *The Garretson Chronicle,* in
which his material and his treatment come nearer to that of
Marquand, shows Brace quite capable of portraying the larger
social pageant of the Garretsons of Compton caught in the
growing up of young Ralph.

The essential differences in attitude between these two
writers remains to be stated. Marquand can be looked upon as a
social novelist (in the older sense of that term—a chronicler of
mores). His underlying attitude beneath the weariness that
surrounds his heroes seems to me to be an ultimate acceptance,
with a sign of *vanitas vanitatum*. Gerald W. Brace writes out of a
more inclusive New England setting. His characters are more
widely representative of the region, and I think it is fair to say as
well that Brace incorporates into his fiction a feel for the locale,
the mountain, or the coastal town as the case may be.

Finally Brace's fiction differs from Marquand's in that the
author of *The Garretson Chronicle* throughout his novels focuses
on the growth of the hero's character via experiential learning.
In this particular trait I feel that Brace is somewhat more closely
aligned with such other novelists of the period as John Steinbeck
or an earlier novelist of New England, Dorothy Canfield Fisher.
When the Bracian hero faces the world of the 1920s he succeeds
or fails largely in relation to the way in which he can adapt by
educating himself toward sensory experience. But this kind of
experience, which has been spoken of in the life of Ralph
Garretson, is often most successfully achieved by New Englanders who pursue their lives some distance from the social or
educational centers. Both Brace and Marquand, however, do

have an urbanity about them. Both are keen observers of the comic irony in human nature. Both have a "classical" dimension. Both practice a good measure of restraint when compared with the more noted American novelists of their era. Brace, I feel, sees in Ralph Garretson a very desirable quality of balance between the old and the new, between the Garretson background and the Kingsley background.

Brace was undoubtedly pleased with the way some of the attempts to "renew" our cities have been carried out. For example, by the work of James Rouse, who is responsible for the Faneuil Hall Marketplace in Boston and the Gallery in Philadelphia. Ralph Garretson became much earlier than men like Rouse the pioneer who was interested in restoring the old and at the same time in maintaining a pride of craftsmanship.

CHAPTER 5

Maine as Utopia

I A Summer's Tale

THE publishing of *The Garretson Chronicle* by W. W. Norton Company marked a significant change in the fortunes of the novelist. Brace's earlier relationship with G. P. Putnam's Sons had been successful enough, but the total sales of his novels had not been too satisfactory. *The Islands* (1936) sold approximately 10,000 copies, but *The Wayward Pilgrims* (1938) and *Light On A Mountain* (1941) slumped downward to approximately 4,000 or 5,000. When Putnam turned down *The Garretson Chronicle* on the basis of a look at its early chapters, Brace turned to W. W. Norton. His manuscript eventually found its way into the hands of a subeditor, George P. Brockway, who urged its publication, expecting not to sell many more copies than *The Wayward Pilgrims* and *The Light On A Mountain* had at Putnam's. But Brockway did like the story and argued with his chief editor that if Norton were going to continue to do any fictional publication, Brace was a good prospect.[1] Eventually the sales of *The Garretson Chronicle* rose to over 50,000 copies.

There were some things about *The Garretson Chronicle* which Brockway thought might be better with modification. These changes were worked out amicably with the author. It marked the beginning of a close friendship that continued through Brace's life. Brockway, a native of Maine, undoubtedly had a more than ordinary sensitivity for the kind of themes that were being handled in the Brace novels. At any rate, over the period dating from approximately January 1947, there began a correspondence which reveals a mutually satisfying relationship that developed as the two began the necessary exchanges of letters about the editing, promotion, and business arrangements for the novel. The later letters indicate that Brockway made many social visits to Deer Isle and to Belmont, Massachusetts, and that Brace often visited Brockway's home in New York. An altogether harmonious relationship developed between the author and his editor.

In *A Summer's Tale* (1949) Brace was returning to the familiar and well-loved coastal area of eastern Maine and its islands. This book contains something more of the contemporary political scene than any book that he wrote, something of the unsettling quality and the fateful experiences of people living during the period of World War II and after. Brace himself, as has been pointed out, was fortunate in having been born too late for military service in 1916–1918 and too early for service in World War II. *A Summer's Tale* cannot be said to be primarily about the war situation; but the general mood and atmosphere of the work, as well as the resolution of main plot, treats warlords and political connivers comically and satirically. This also is the most unusual of the Brace novels in its formal structuring. A description by Edward Wagenknecht, Brace's colleague at Boston University, can serve as an introduction to this fifth novel: "In *A Summer's Tale*, which takes place on an imaginary island off the coast of Maine, we have the ultimate expression of Brace's worship of islands and also the best example of what a 'summer novel' has come to be like in a thoughtful and troubled age. *A Summer's Tale* is utopia, comic opera, a tale of derring-do, and a local color piece. It embraces a burlesque on fifth columnists, journalists, and the American Navy, and it is a highly romantic love story with echoes of the great verses of Spenser and Sir Thomas Wyatt sounding through its cadenced prose."[2]

II   *Penobscot History*

Penobscot Bay and the islands thereabouts where Brace had summered since his early boyhood play a rich role in the annals of early European exploration of the New England coast. In the 1500s Spanish, Basque, and Portuguese fishermen used the islands off the Maine coast as campsites for processing their catch. Cabot and Verrazano made early claims for England and for France. Raleigh and Sir Humphrey Gilbert followed with voyages aimed directly at exploring the coast of Maine. Before that, John Walker took possession of the area about Penobscot Bay as early as 1580. The famous Norembega myth, which told of

a great and rich city—greater and richer than even some of the
places sacked by the Spaniards—was at times conceived as lying
in the vicinity of just such a river as the Penobscot. Sir Fernando
Gorgas, a Sommersetshire English man (despite the Latin name),
persistently tried to colonize the Maine coast in the early 1600s
before Jamestown and Plymouth colonies were settled. Scurvy
often led to defeat in these ventures.

Earlier than the British efforts, however, were those of the
Frenchman Pierre Du Gast, the Sieur de Monts. Jesuits such as
Pierre Biard and Ennemond Masse joined Du Gast in his efforts
to settle at Mount Desert. This small colony seemed to be doing
fairly well in its relationship with the Indians when Sir Samuel
Argalls came upon them. He burned the mission in 1613 and took
the French, Fr. Biard, and the converted Indians as captives.
Those that he could, Argalls sold into slavery; some that were set
adrift in small boats made their way to Port Royal. It was the first
direct conflict of French and British in the New World, and it is
against this historical backdrop that Brace works out his *A
Summer's Tale*.[3]

The hero of the narrative is Anthony Wyatt, a writer and a
freelance lecturer. The time is June. In the opening scene in
Camden Harbor, Anthony Wyatt is making last-minute preparations before boarding his sloop *The Doubloon* for a vacation
cruise off the Maine coastline. He is importuned by the crew of a
great black diesel yacht, *Typee* (named for Herman Melville's
first novel about a tropical paradise), which pulls in between the
wharf and *The Doubloon*, pushing his small skiff under the piles.
The owners of the yacht, and their family, however, appear to be
a gracious group. They are Mr. Theodore Marquis; his wife,
Prudence; three sons, seventeen to twenty-three years old; and
two daughters—Beverly, fifteen, and June, about twenty-two.
June's "golden, blue-eyed fineness"—her pale gold hair and sea-
blue eyes with quick smile register with Anthony, who half
kiddingly asks if June will join him on his sailing trip. She demurs
on the grounds that her father thinks sailing dangerous. But the
Marquis family extends a general invitation to visit them.
Anthony is warned that the approach to August Island is difficult.
He gets directions from the *Typee*'s Captain Bunker, who tells
him it lies a distance southeast of Matinicus Rock and is usually
surrounded by fog.

A month later, working his way northeast as he puts into

various small harbors to write and loaf about, Anthony loses his bearings. A gusty northeast gale drives *The Doubloon* into the open Maine Gulf. Fog and wind continue the next day. Evening with more squalls finds him beyond the outermost islands of the Maine Gulf until his sloop is driven upon rock. Like Crusoe he wakes to find himself on a smooth pebble beach. He begins to explore the uncharted island. Despite its rugged reefs and stretch of wild coast, a mile's walk inland reveals fresh forest, pasture land, fields and clear beautiful air. He falls asleep exhausted and dreams of the terrible sounds of *The Doubloon* smashing against rock. He awakes to June Marquis's "Are you all right?" Her face "seemed like a steady light, eyes blue and clear, creamy skin made golden by summer suns."

Anthony learns that August Island is uncharted and unrecognized by either the United States or Canada. Island gravestone markers show dates as old as 1702 with the name of Emile Byard. On their way to the Marquis home they stop for a refreshment at Mrs. Byard's stone house, built in 1547. She has five sons. Theodore Marquis later explains to Anthony how the island was occupied by the French voyagers. There are Argalls, too, among the present dwellers. Theodore stresses the religious motivation of the French and the piratelike tactics of their British rivals who seemed more intent on business opportunities than on anything else. At present, Mr. Marquis rules the Island, as head of a council of three. The island had been legally granted to his family, the Bourbon line, but for a century the Marquises paid no attention to rents and the world forgot August Island—until the émigrés from the French Revolution took up residence there. Since that time the Marquises have kept up their fortune chiefly by marrying heiresses from Boston, thus sustaining the wonderful chateau and their giant yacht. Anthony gives his own pedigree— a Boston actress for a grandmother who married a writer named Wyatt, who claimed descent from Sir Thomas Wyatt, the sixteenth century poet. Both died in poverty and starvation. Anthony's father wanted to make a scholar out of him, but he became a sports reporter, a wartime camp journalist, and at present is a freelance lecturer and short-story writer. The modern Marquises always have a fair number of guests brought back and forth from Boston by the *Typee*, especially during the August season. Norman and Celia Mount (last of the line of Sieur de Monts) work for Theodore as waitress and engineer. People

like the Mounts live on the island year round, but the Marquis
family seldom does. Son Lowell, twenty-three, an ornithologist,
appears to Anthony as the only Marquis without graciousness. He
is off to Boston to visit a group of his friends—the Committee on
National Economy. Milton is about nineteen and athletic;
Winthrop is of slighter build but wittier, chattier, and more
bookish. Beverly, fifteen, is at times all blond loveliness and yet
at other moments all boisterous banter.

As in Shakespeare's *The Tempest* philosophical conversation is
the vogue at island gatherings. June reminds Anthony at
breakfast that swimming at high tide means going without suits.
Mr. Marquis explains: "We try to live Rousseauistically. . . . It is
easy to push theory into folly, so we don't insist. But the family
has been brought up to question any sort of affectation."
Anthony begins to feel that the race of gods the Greeks had
imagined for Mount Olympus would be more at home on August
Island.

Anthony's rival for June Marquis is young Sam Argall. He is
powerfully formed, with thick chest. "He held himself solidly,
and seemed to turn his body whenever he turned his head; the
eyes were grey and unrevealing, half-hidden under their brows."
Sam and Milton play doubles tennis against June and Anthony.
Anthony senses a deep hostility from Sam for whom June holds a
kind of proprietary rather than a romantic feeling.

Sam Argall offers to take a look at the wreckage of *The
Doubloon* with June and Anthony. It turns out that Sam is more
intent on harming Anthony than on doing him a favor. Sam
wrecks his own craft when he attempts to drown Anthony. Both
June and Anthony risk their own safety, and have to use violence
upon Sam to get him safely to shore. Anthony realizes that Sam's
love for June motivated his crazy behavior at the wreckage. He
confronts June with his view and learns that June's fondness for
Sam appears to be based simply on their growing up together on
the island.

Meanwhile, a United States Navy destroyer appears unexpec-
tedly and anchors menacingly just three miles off August Island.
It spoils the merrymaking mood for Captain Bunker's son's
wedding party at the schoolhouse. The captain speaks for all the
islanders: "The Government's got no right here; we don't belong
to anyone but ourselves. They better not try anything, by God."

Meanwhile Lowell's guests arrive. They are an odd assortment of pretentious political activists. They include Mr. Doremus, who is short, stout, and reserved, with large features—"an unnaturally solemn Mr. Punch." (It turns out that he and Anthony have verbally crossed swords elsewhere.) Mrs. Oliphant has a kind of petrified appearance. She is the author of *The Menace of Anarchy,* which no one but Lowell takes seriously. With them also are Paul Sevill ("a tall young gentleman in salmon pink flowers, tweed jacket and white knotted scarf and ironic smile") and his companion Miss Carla, "well painted and curled with black hair to her shoulders and a long filmy gown of palest green."

Doremus is the financial backer of this group of conspirators; Anthony warns Marquis to take them seriously. Their essential plot is a fantastic one: to make Lowell, a Bourbon, the king of France. Lowell and Anthony clash; he requests Anthony's dismissal from August Island. Anthony announces his intentions of doing just that, but first he formally makes it known to Mr. Marquis that he desires to marry June. Lowell tries to laugh this matter out of court; Mr. Marquis, a bit taken back, affirms June shall marry whom she pleases.

Milton Marquis offers Anthony his sloop, the *Posy,* as a gift. It is a finer boat than *The Doubloon* and Anthony, completely in love with the craft, buys it. June accompanies him on a trial sail. " 'It's like that first moment when lovers fully reveal themselves', he said, smiling at his extravagance, 'The barriers come down, the clothes come off—it's the end of one life and the beginning of another.' " Anthony shifts the topic to June herself and proclaims his adoration of her. He ponders the duration of the happiness he has found in the past few days. June realizes that the real fear Anthony has about Lowell and his friends is that for him they are a symptom of the world's unhappiness crowding close to August Island. June reassures him of the Marquis family's friendship. Anthony very deliberately begins to quote in full Sir Thomas Wyatt's poem "They Flee from Me That Sometime Did Me Seek."

June shows some fear of the poem and the way Anthony recited it. It was like an invitation to "a dark world of passion." Anthony says that, although he feels Sir Thomas was a cynic about women, he didn't invent passion. He admits he has been playing a "dark and calculated game" with her ever since she glanced back over her shoulder as she led him to the Marquis

home after his shipwreck. She is afraid she may be only another
of Anthony's metaphors in all this, but she is willing to consider
his proposition. But she wants some time. Anthony persists. He is
ready to leave August Island in the *Posy* and he wants her to go
with him. As the two return, there is further trouble with
Doremus and Lowell over Anthony's being with June. Anthony is
forced to knock a gun from Doremus's hand, while June knocks
Lowell over the head with a broom handle.

The business of the destroyer in the harbor is made clear.
Captain Ketcham gives an ultimatum to the islanders: the navy
must pursue a test program and the Island must be cleared of its
inhabitants by August 24. Mr. Marquis readies the *Typee* to sail to
Boston and Washington to seek aid. Anthony suddenly decides to
go along. His strategy is to seek the services of an old journalist
friend, Maud Miller, an experienced political columnist, the
crusading sort who loves to join a good fight. Sam Argall sculls
out to the destroyer after dark and dynamites a fair-sized hole in
its hull. The sailors arrest Sam and put him under surveillance.
The islanders are not to leave. They hold a council of war. Maud
Miller's first articles present the August Islanders as man's last
hope for freedom on the globe. For better or worse her pen has
made the Island everybody's business. It is too late to turn back
now.

The close of the story centers on Sam's escape from August
Island. Anthony and June attempt to secrete Sam aboard the
Typee after navy inspection. The three miss rendezvous with the
Typee. Then in the darkness they head northeast. With Sam
asleep, June confides to Anthony that she could never be Sam's
woman because what he wants is an occasional woman. She
hesitates and finally agrees to go with Anthony "anywhere."
The three reach Machias Bay in rain and blinding fog. When
Anthony goes ashore for provisions, he learns from a townsman
that the *Posy* with Sam at the helm has headed east without him.
He sleeps the night in the open and in the morning comes upon
June, who had jumped the sloop and swam ashore when Sam
headed for Canada. That evening the two consummate their
love.

The next day it is Anthony who brings up the question of
formal marriage. June defers to him: "Whatever you think is
proper." June feels that

I always thought it would be complicated and serious and scary, but it isn't. You poets sort of make it sound like that, with your dark passions—as though it had to be sinful. We aren't sinful, Tony. (p. 254)

When they return to August Island, they slip once more past the *Typee*. Mr. Marquis has some misgivings about their "marriage." When he asks about their license, June replies that they felt he could do that part; their vows had already been exchanged. She reminds her father of his own principles of virtue before convention. Mr. Marquis is persuaded to do the ceremony.

Maud Miller's campaign in the press has worked wonders. August Island is declared free. Lowell and his company are disgraced. The only real concern for all is that the peace of August Island will now suffer from the notoriety. Treasure hunters have already poured in to seek the rumored gold. August Island will have to join the modern world for better or for worse. The *Posy* sails westward, "diminished to a small spire against the vast golden twilight."

III *The Critical Reception*

Reviewers of *A Summer's Tale* took rather kindly to the new note of fantasy in Brace. Edward Weeks in the *Atlantic* generally liked the lyrical quality of the descriptions of the island. "I read the book for its pleasant make-believe, and with curiosity to see how the author would work out the triangle with Anthony, June and Sam." Weeks had some serious reservations, however, about some of the dialogue and also with the "irrelevancy" of the political subplot. He ended his review by quoting Anthony from the novel: "I think the oldest of mortal dreams . . . is the blessed isle where folk live in peace and beauty, and the women are all fair and no man is deceived. This must be it."[4]

An unsigned reviewer in the *New Yorker* wrote: "This Down East Idyll has a glancing resemblance to innumerable utopian chronicles but lacks the didactic quality of most of them. . . . Mr. Brace wisely makes no attempt at either credibility or sermonizing, and his offshore excursion is both urbane and satisfyingly romantic."[5]

C. V. Terry in the *New York Times Book Review* called the mood a modern *Tempest* . . . "a lighter-than-air commedia dell'arte . . . a cast whose resemblance to the people of a certain famous comedy is not accidental, social comment that (on occasion) comes off brilliantly—and a romance that never fails to charm even in its more lyrical moments. This reviewer felt that Brace did not permit any moral to weigh down the pace, or any philosophical strain as well. "One closes the book with the conviction that Mr. Brace's Atlantic Eden is none the worse for its brush with the U.S.A.—and that it will keep its character intact, even when next summer tourists descend in droves."[6]

IV *The Moral Quest*

There is much in *A Summer's Tale* that might be considered a kind of holiday of the creative imagination. It was the author's first and last effort in the realm of fantasy. Perhaps it is wrong to take it as offering serious reflection upon man's existence. Certainly it should not be taken as Shakespeare's *Tempest* often is—the most serious kind of philosophizing about the nature of man by a writer who is thought to be conscious of his laying aside his creative art and about to enter into retirement. On the other hand, Brace's manner of loosely echoing other writers such as Melville, Shakespeare, and Sydney and his naming his hero after the sixteenth-century poet Wyatt, cannot be brushed aside as merely whimsical borrowings. It is also fair to say that for all fancifulness and romantic stress in the novel there is a strong undercurrent of serious moral import in the action of *A Summer's Tale*. That this aspect of the story does not interfere or burden the romance is a large tribute to the writer's skill.

The amount of time spent on introducing us to the background of the early settlers of the island in their intrigues and the description of their offspring seems designed to have the reader realize that people are still pretty much the same wherever you find them, even though the courtly manners may have sharply diminished. What Brace also is implying is that the bonds of *camaraderie* and friendship are still present in the modern world—and one often finds these qualities in Maine communities. Brace speaks eloquently of these traits in his book on Maine, *Between Wind and Water:*

The democratic and communal habit has little theoretical or self-conscious basis; it exists as the natural outcome of old conditions. Some of it is based simply on good character, or on what the moral anarchists of our time would condemn as puritanism—assuming that any stern ethical code is an evil; actually the early puritan rigors of the Boston region never controlled the people of Maine, whose codes were firm and practical rather than doctrinal and tinged with madness. They lived, the down-easters, in a state of mutual respect and cooperation partly because they were good people to begin with, and partly because the pioneering work of settling, cutting forests, clearing land, building and using boats, could be better done with communal good will. . . . But as to character itself, what can be said? The 'goodness' existed among them as a code, as it did among all the New England pioneers: it was based on the unquestioned belief in Christian ethics and the omnipotence of God.[7]

When the islanders repel the "invasion" of the government in the form of a navy destroyer, Brace is reasserting the common sense of the folk. History tells of the earlier episode of the *Margaretta*, a British cutter anchored off Machias Bay shortly before the Revolution. The Machias people were fed up with the way the British had been behaving and they took matters into their own hands, captured the frigate and turned it over to authorities in Boston. It is commonly referred to as the first naval engagement of the Revolution. It was a spirit similar to that with which Dorothy Canfield Fisher endowed a Vermont community in her *Seasoned Timber* (1939). The small town rises to the occasion and throws off a fascist movement in the form of anti-Semitism which threatens to turn their academy into an "exclusive" school.

The attempts upon Anthony's life by Sam Argall as well as the plottings against him on the part of Lowell, Doremus, and Mrs. Oliphant are melodramatically real, just as the love that Anthony discovers for June Marquis is real. Ironically the very stratagem he employs to expose the conspirators and to save the islanders from governmental interference involves use of the power of the press. This exploitation of the power of the press (in itself another questionable modern agency in certain respects) is no doubt in keeping with Anthony Wyatt's presumed ancestor, Sir Thomas Wyatt, who was also known for his ability at court intrigues in the time of Henry VIII.

But the main quest of Anthony Wyatt is best seen in terms of wisdom, moral wisdom. This may seem a strange statement in the light of all the romance, the melodrama and the pleasure that the reader is afforded in this novel. Clearly, however, Brace would

have the reader follow the adventures of Anthony in order to see
in his actions something that is clearly apart from the ways of the
world as witnessed in such people as Sam Argall, Lowell Marquis
and others. The moral wisdom implied in the actions of Anthony
Wyatt is compatible with the ideas of Sir Philip Sydney and
Edmund Spenser, although Brace is not holding out an ideal of
moral behavior as is found in *Arcadia* or in *The Fairie Queen*.
The poem of Wyatt which Anthony quotes to June in the *Posy* is
noteworthy for its calm approach to honest love and passion for a
woman. June Marquis tends to shy away from Anthony's honest
passion. She sees its darker aspects primarily. Perhaps her
scientific training (she is a medical student who returns to her
school at the end of the story) arouses her suspicions of him. But
it is through Anthony's poetic insights that the truth of their
relationship is made known. Actually the two leave August Island
to complete their courtship and to consummate their love. The
Posy is a particularly well-chosen name for the sloop that
Anthony acquires from Milton Marquis. In Elizabethan times it
referred to a verse of poetry inscribed within a ring or upon a
knife blade. In *A Summer's Tale* it comes to stand for a way of
life, the kind Anthony Wyatt pursues, trying to understand the
great forces operating in human existence, trying to harmonize
them in his own life, trying to use knowledge and wisdom in his
relationship with other people.

If we make some loose analogies with *The Tempest* of
Shakespeare and *A Summer's Tale*, it is necessary to see Anthony
more in the role of Prospero, perhaps, than that of Ferdinand,
although as lover Anthony shares in the latter's role. Theodore
Marquis, on the other hand, has no particular affinity for magic.
He does, however, show a little of Prospero's concern for a
daughter's welfare, and he does seek justice for all concerned on
the island. Prospero's source of power was his books, his liberal
studies. Theodore Marquis has a liberal philosophical approach
but Anthony's hand is most important in the shaping of the events
in the story, even though he has been the one cast up on the
shore of August Island. He knows the power of the modern
public-relations journalism as well as its grossnesses. He uses it
very tellingly to help subdue the evils that envelop the island.
Sam Argall is the closest resemblance we have to a Caliban in the
story. It is interesting that Brace has him vanish into the
Canadian province of New Brunswick to avoid any further clash

with the United States Navy. Like his counterpart in *The Tempest,* Sam has flirted with the island conspirators as Caliban had allied himself to Trinculo and Stephano. Lowell Marquis becomes a kind of usurping nobleman with his group of supporters. Instead of an Ariel as in *The Tempest* we have Anthony's imagination and powers of reason to help steer the action.

Brace's turn of plot, which allows Anthony and June to effect their "marriage" without benefit of clergy, actually serves to focus on the moral nature of marriage itself. The love between the two is certainly of an honorable kind. The love scenes, delightfully convincing and well managed, become a commentary upon the more sensationalized love-making in the run of modern stories.

Mr. Lary is a sort of unofficial minister of August Island. He is an aspiring writer who keeps a small general store near the shore. He has written an article called "The Christian Spirit." Half apologetically he tells Anthony Wyatt that the islanders are Christians. They engage in a brief but quite philosophical exchange on the problem of evil. Mr. Lary argues that evil exists of necessity because "otherwise good would have no meaning for us. . . . The worst evil seems to be intellectual, a product of man's superior intelligence—mind without spirit. You can call it Satan if you like, but I prefer to consider it simply one of the conditions of life which it is my duty to change." Anthony encourages Mr. Lary in his writing and tries to point out to him that the forms of writing have changed and editors are not sympathetic to his religious essays even though Anthony admits that their "truth is as valid as ever." Anthony believes a man must "reach the imagination first, and through that the understanding." This is what *A Summer's Tale* seeks to do for the reader.

Finally, it should also be noted that Walter Scott's novel *The Pirate* (1822), which was about the Orkney and Shetland Islands off the northern coast of Scotland, was also a kind of inspiration for the author in addition to *The Tempest.* Brace says in his unpublished second volume of autobiographic memoirs that the Scott novel contained the lines "Oh were there an island . . . that should anchor in heaven." These words were a kind of motif "that played romantically through my early life in the days when we lived on Mill Island."[8]

In the same context Brace wrote that it was the real-life Porter family from a neighboring island that gave him his model for the Marquis family of the story. Evidently it was their great spirit of happiness and mutual affection that Brace admired to the point of trying to capture it in his tale. "They never doubted the worth of their effort to attain virtue and beauty," he tells us, and apparently they lived in comfort and security, too.[9]

This kind of people, cultural aristocrats, fascinated the novelist. However, as we shall see, his novels take on, more and more, a darker pigmentation as they move closer to the post-World War II scene. Perhaps *A Summer's Tale* may best be described as a final interlude of essentially romantic fantasy before Brace's stories begin to give us a much harsher New England scene.

CHAPTER 6

The World of Wyndham

IN 1952 Gerald Brace's sixth novel appeared, *The Spire*. It presented some new facets of his imagination and might be loosely called an academic novel in the sense that it portrayed mainly life in a small college town in contemporary New England. For the first time the professor-novelist chose to train his sights chiefly upon the academic world, although frequently in the other stories the academic world had appeared as a significant part of the hero's background as in *Light on a Mountain* and *The Garretson Chronicle*. In his last novel, *The Department* (1968), he was to return successfully, again, to the academic scene as a primary focus.

Brace calls his fictional college Wyndham, the name given to Henry Gaunt's college in *Light on a Mountain*. Wyndham in that novel most readily suggested Dartmouth because of its proximity to the Gaunt's home in southern Vermont. In *The Spire* Wyndham is located in Western Massachusetts, about ninety miles from where Professor Henry Gaunt came from in Vermont. For the reader of *The Spire* it is, of course, not essential that any particular likeness to a small New England liberal arts college be assumed. (Brace's Wyndham is not to be confused with Windham College, Putney, Vt. 1951–1978) Brace was giving his readers a composite of such schools as Williams, Amherst, Dartmouth, and Mount Holyoke—where he had taught previously. At the time of the writing of *The Spire* Brace was teaching at Boston University. His dedication reads: "TO MY COLLEAGUES—Who live, love, labor freely, nor discuss a brother's right to freedom."

The novel's action unfolds during a single academic year— from Henry Gaunt's arrival one June for an interview for a position in the English Department to the following June, when he makes his decision to leave Wyndham. It is told in the third person, with Henry Gaunt always in the center of focus. The college calendar provides, with its seasonal ceremonies and functions, many natural points for dramatic emphasis, and Brace, writing with an insider's knowledge of such institutional rhythms, writes very skillfully about the English Department meeting; the general faculty meeting; the faculty dinner party; and similar occasions.

I   *The Return of Henry Gaunt*

Henry Gaunt (we saw him in the earlier novel going off to Columbia graduate school) is now thirty-seven, a widower with a five-year-old son whose mother had died in childbirth. Henry met his wife at Columbia. She said she was seeking both a scholarly career and a husband. Petite and well organized, she had consciously given her life to save her infant's. Henry had taught first at Geneva, then at Texas University, and had authored a book called *American Gothic* which had given him a good reputation in American literature circles. It had given him the opportunity to come back to New England to be nearer his small boy, who was living with Sylvia, his sister in Vermont. President Gidney of Wyndham had been a colleague of Henry's at Texas. He lets Henry know that if he accepts the position offered, the chairman's post will be his the following year: he will replace the retiring McAdam. Gidney is frank about Wyndham. He has a fight on his hands with the trustees over fiscal policy. He would like to upgrade the academic standards as well and he thinks Henry's Vermont virtues can help carry out difficult decisions in regard to some of the older men.

Miss Lizzie Houghton is Gidney's secretary. She is twenty-nine, with a "plainness that was part of her design. The pale amber hair was pulled straight back into a knot. She wore no make-up or decorations, and her grey cotton seersucker dress hung limply. Yet if she were fixed in marble, he thought, she would do well as a Grecian deity." Gaunt is attracted to her as much by her appearance as by her attitude, which is self-assured but with an exaggerated coldness despite his best efforts to be pleasant to her. Her rare smile reminds him of his late wife.

Henry finds lodgings at Miss Jamison's, a garrulous but generous woman who had turned down an opportunity for marriage, perhaps because she was influenced by the atmosphere of the college to expect something more in a man than her hometown beau offered. Between Miss Jamison's friendship and, eventually, Lizzie Houghton's, Henry Gaunt is afforded, without seeking it, two centers of information about what is current in the town and on the campus. But Wyndham the town and Wyndham the campus are not neatly separated; they are more nearly identical.

The politics of the English Department clarifies itself at an early meeting held at McAdam's home. Greg Flanders asserts himself. He is the man with an established reputation from his publications, and he has a temperament to go with it. He likes to name-drop, with a flourish of his cigarette, about his connections with scholars at other universities. Bill Pinney is another older teacher but without a portfolio of publications. He is allergic to Greg Flanders's stuffiness. He speaks his mind freely about academic pettifogging in any of its forms. Flanders is forty-five; Bill Pinney, fifty-six. Henry Gaunt plays it down the middle, trying sensibly not to make any alliances until he has seen more of Wyndham.

Another reason for Henry's coming to Wyndham is that it brings him closer to research materials on Thomas Gale, an important minor writer in American Literature—"a sort of missing link between Poe and Hawthorne—a Puritan obsessed by baroque romanticism, a death-intoxicated Yankee, a fantastic decadent imprisoned in classic New England. . . . He drank, he lusted, he shot himself—in a word, he was a poet" (pp. 84–85).[1] Henry wanted to do a full biography of this man, some of whose papers were thought still to be somewhere in Wyndham; Mrs. Dudley, Gale's granddaughter and one of the reigning ladies of the town, was known, in fact, to have some of Gale's papers. Greg Flanders also has claims in Gale scholarship, with three published articles on the poet.

Henry learns that Thomas Gale had lived once where Lizzie Houghton now lives with her father, an ex-professor, and her brother Bert, a student at the college. When he suggests to Lizzie that he would like to look around her home, she balks at the idea. She hints at scandalous events associated with her family, some of which Henry had already heard about. As Henry is walking Lizzie home, they meet Mr. Houghton aimlessly rambling in his speech. Henry accepts the awkward situation and invites himself to stay for supper over Lizzie's strong protestations. Houghton's reputation has become tarnished because of stories of his being too free in showing his affections to some teenaged girls. Even though the stories had been exaggerated, he was forced to resign his post. Always he talked of his return to teaching mathematics.

At Greg Flanders's dinner party there is more talk about Lizzie having been in prison. Mrs. Dudley is chief purveyor of gossip. Finally, Miss Jamison clarifies the case of Lizzie for Henry Gaunt. Ten years ago she had an affair with a college student resulting in pregnancy. What complicated matters was Lizzie's living in the old Gale house at the moment when a big anniversary of the poet was being celebrated. When Mrs. Dudley tried to pretend to visitors that there was no such place, she more or less forced herself into a position of becoming an enemy of Lizzie; she preferred charges of immorality against Lizzie. Hattie Dudley took out some of her wrath on Lizzie.

College politics simmer as the semester goes along. President Gidney calls on Henry in an anxious state of mind over Dean Markham's threatened resignation. The issue is over Gidney's pressuring for Professor Bucke's early retirement. Dean Markham was the living symbol of the old Wyndham tradition, and he did not want to see his old friend Bucke pressured. Gidney maneuvers to the point of asking Henry to take Markham's deanship. Henry at first recoils, but he does realize Gidney is making an honest effort to improve the college; Henry promises serious consideration.

Henry encounters increasing stubbornness and resistance in his attempts to develop his interest in Lizzie. At a concert Lizzie first mentions her baby being born in prison and dying there. She speaks of being in love with the young man and not looking ahead to any consequences. Henry confides to her his affection for his dead wife, Susan. He admits it may not have been the kind of love that Lizzie shared with her man. At first Lizzie had wanted to take on the whole town in a fight to the finish, but the odds were extreme, especially because of the burden of her father's plight. The town won easily.

Henry accepts the dean's job with provisions that he can return to his teaching position after a fair trial. At Thanksgiving in Vermont, Sylvia's warmth continues to strike Lizzie. Her home is a combination of thriving rascally youngsters and modern conveniences, since her husband runs an appliance store. Lizzie begins to bend a little. They all drive up Stafford Mountain to persuade Grandpa Gaunt to come down from his cabin for a holiday dinner. The old man resists stubbornly; Henry thinks the place has the smell of death about it. He reminds Lizzie that his mother had helped to build life with her creative instincts; Mr. Gaunt merely exists, makes do with anything that is left over.

Henry faces some rough reactions from the faculty over Bucke's early retirement. He goes to New York to face a screening by the college's board of trustees. The board is persuaded that his appointment doesn't mean the end of Wyndham's ideals. Henry now plunges into his full responsibilities: special requests of students; reports of curriculum committees; a new chairman for English; the resignation of the football coach, who claims that Wyndham is not being competitive; urgent letters from parents charging racial discrimination; alumni charges of Communist sympathizers on the faculty—as well as behavior codes for the spring house parties.

Greg Flanders calls on the dean and has a plan worked out by which he offers himself as chairman for English. He is maneuvering because he feels Bill Pinney might be appointed chairman by the president. It is Henry's first test. He politely listens to Flanders but lets him know that Gidney and himself have agreed to offer the post to Jenks, the present chairman of Freshman English. Flanders stomps out, calling him a liar.

Lizzie is a guest at a party at Gidney's. Entertainment centers on some charades that have been rehearsed and costumed. Lizzie to everyone's surprise gets high praise with her acting out of "Wyrd." The idea catches on that she is the one to play Lady Macbeth in a special dedication performance for a new theater arts building. She for the moment abandons herself to her success.

Henry Gaunt disagrees with President Gidney that the college should encourage men such as Flanders to stay on when it is very apparent, at least to Henry, that Flanders is a source of unhappiness for his colleagues. Gidney wants Flanders for his publications. Henry insists that he will work towards his own goals but he will give Gidney proper notice before acting on any such matters. Gidney doesn't lose his composure even when Henry tells him that like many administrators he has lost the human touch. Henry's offer of resignation is turned down.

In May Lizzie and Henry drive into the country. Lizzie is again in poor spirits and pale. Lizzie fights off Henry's hand as he tries to comfort her. Later Henry professes his love. Lizzie pleads that he not pursue matters. When Henry speaks of marriage she shakes her head. She admits her love but considers marriage impossible given Wyndham gossip and her family situation. As she leaves him at her home she breaks for the door and shuts Henry outside.

At Mrs. Dudley's dinner party Henry Gaunt brings up the matter of the poet Thomas Gale's papers, some of which are in Mrs. Dudley's possession. She tells Henry that she is studying the materials and will decide which are suitable to keep. Mrs. Dudley seems more interested in her niece Angela's relationship with the dean of Wyndham than she is in having Gaunt see the Gale papers. Henry promises to return later to the Dudley home to see if Hattie has made up her mind about the papers and to view Angela's painting on glass.

Henry uses Miss Jamison as a sounding board about marrying Lizzie. She thinks it an indiscretion that will cause endless repercussions in the community, but when Henry mentions love she remarks, "Well in that case you'll just have to—." A visit to Lizzie follows. She is in a sullen temper. Henry encourages her to throw a few objects. When her mood has cooled, the subject turns again to marriage. After her "yes" is said, "she smiled with more tenderness than he had ever seen in her face."

Henry lets President Gidney know right away of the impending loss of his valuable secretary. Gidney is currently beset with the problem of an investigation by one of the members of the Board of Trustees, Mr. Garvin. Gidney had been sidestepping the curriculum committee's report and the reason is now apparent. Garvin is not sympathetic to new expenditures. Henry finds out that the new Theater Arts Building has been largely the promotion of Greg Flanders; it is being paid for by Flanders's friends, thus pressuring the college into a new full-time drama man. Henry still tries vainly to get Gidney to see that the vanity of Flanders is a real detriment to the college.

Henry at last gets to view the Gale papers at Mrs. Dudley's, after he has dutifully seen Angela's paintings. The Gale material does appear important to him, especially the unpublished poems. He advises Mrs. Dudley to seek Flanders's advice; he realizes his own course now lies away from Wyndham and Thomas Gale. Mrs. Dudley says this move will destroy him.

Academic affairs reach a showdown at the last English Department meeting of the year with both Henry and Gidney in attendance. Henry suggests that the department elect its own chairman, to effect a greater harmony. Gidney calls this idea impractical and hastens to announce that Flanders will be the new acting head of English. Henry has one more suggestion. He knows a young teacher in Oregon with good promise of scholarship in Dickens. His writing has not been critically fashionable and his degree is merely a Bachelor of Science. But Henry feels he would do well at Wyndham. Flanders inevitably pushes for his own candidate, a new PhD from Yale who has been working on the dating of Shakespeare's plays. Henry's frustrations have now reached an impasse.

The long-awaited production of *Macbeth,* geared to the commencement week festivities and the centennial of America's first college theater society at Wyndham, is approaching. When Lizzie talks of her marriage with Henry she again shows her hidden fears. She is aware that the tensions between her boss, Gidney, and his old colleague, her fiancé, have something to do with her engagement. Her younger brother, Bertie, rankling under old family grievances against Mrs. Dudley and hearing of her attitudes, now, toward his sister's marriage, takes out his hostilities by firing rocks through Mrs. Dudley's windows, about seventeen of them. He is apprehended and must go to the state hospital for observation.

The performance of *Macbeth* goes well enough in Bill Pinney's cut version. Liz is tense, as Sylvia, Henry's sister, observes to him, before the play: ". . . As the scene built she seemed to relish it; her smile had a demon look to it, as though the terrible words were the very ones she was meant to utter." Lizzie's performance is a large success. But when Henry tries to find her after the final curtain when she is not present with the other actors for the calls, she cannot be located. Finally he sees her standing on the ledge of one of the concrete piers of the town bridge. She did not respond to his call. He manages to pull her down onto his shoulders and work his way back through the deeper water to the grass. On the way back to Miss Jamison's boarding house Lizzie says simply: "I didn't know what to do." It was apparent to Henry that she had in mind to take her own life.

Miss Jamison's seven-year-old applejack brandy revived her. Lizzie tells Henry that she had been making a plan for some time. It had become a part of her dreaming but she had failed, succumbing to a mass of fears. Henry prefers to call the matter a "needed lesson in what it means to be moral." She is taken to

Vermont to recuperate. Wedding plans are set for late July. Lizzie's sister, Abbie, takes over the care of Mr. Houghton who is moved into an apartment in a nearby town after the house is sold, with the promise of some help from Henry, who has accepted a teaching position at a Technical Institute in the West. Henry also promises assistance for young Bertie. As Henry drives out of Wyndham towards Vermont when he has completed his last academic chores for the semester, he looks back on the college. His perception is: "The little hill was like a green island and the arrow point of the spire stood up in the center like a hope fulfilled and sanctified and half forgotten. It was all a unit there, a visible institution, well founded and secure and fortified against time; seen all at once like this, rising in the sky above its hill of trees, it gathered an almost feudal serenity and complacence like some sacred mount of the Middle Ages" (pp. 377-378).

II   *The Human Comedy*

The Spire differs from earlier Brace novels in several important aspects. The protagonist, Henry Gaunt, is thirty-nine years old. He is not a young university man making his way in the world; Gaunt is a seasoned hero. His significant publication *American Gothic* ushers him into the academic world on secure footing with his Wyndham associates, even those with greater seniority. He has faced personal suffering in his loss of his wife. In seeking a new life, he has separated himself from his son, David, only temporarily.

Second, Brace in *The Spire* is drawing a world in which he had been thoroughly immersed for over twenty years. The world of Wyndham College is made up primarily of recognizable universal types to be found in any college in America. The author's feel for this academic world is unerringly true, and not merely reflective of the small New England liberal-arts college. The main characters of the story, Lizzie and Henry Gaunt, are native New Englanders; Fred Gidney, Greg Flanders, and many other important figures are not. All in all, *The Spire* is a canvas more crowded than any novel that Brace had previously written; it has more characters with more diverse traits. An important aspect of the novel is the interrelationship of town and gown. There are the tensions that traditionally arise between these entities, but they are not the most significant ones created in the novel. The moral tensions that arise within the life at Wyndham are the significant ones.

The Spire is a more comprehensive reading by Brace of New England life than his earlier work in the sense that it juxtaposes the larger intellectual world of the college located physically in the midst of the smaller world of the town. Henry Gaunt encompasses the two worlds and is successful in each in overcoming the difficulties that he faces. His Vermont background as recorded in the earlier novel makes us aware that his values were grounded in his love of the farm and the neighboring mountains and that his relationship with his parents and his brother and sister was based on a considered reasonableness. Henry Gaunt as dean shows the flowering of this personal integrity. The manner in which Henry handles the round of tensions and conflicts in both the college affairs and in his personal life reveals him as a rather uncommon hero. Brace's implications here seem quite clear. It is a veiw that might be described as pastoral in its basic conception. The kind of chivalric behavior and vision seen in Henry Gaunt is spawned from two sources: He has good native virtues from the rural upbringing and this has been heightened by his diligent pursuit of the intellectual life, but never pursued for its own sake or in neglect of the human needs. That is why when he finds the poseur, the weaklings and the spiritually crippled he handles these human elements with an unusual amount of composure and compassion. There is irony here in Henry's departure after only one year at Wyndham with such promise.

The Spire shows us the pastoral reflex again at work in the novels of Gerald W. Brace. In the final analysis Wyndham College is a kind of ideal that the author is presenting for us in the midst of a modern world fairly bankrupt of values. That ideal should be grounded in the simpler and old-fashioned virtues that Brace feels were once cherished and are somehow lost. The world of Wyndham is struggling, but aside from Henry Gaunt there doesn't seem to be much direction to its life.

It would be well at this point to make use of an extended quotation from chapter eight to give the reader a chance to examine Brace's handling of the Wyndham scene. The setting is Professor Greg Flanders's house. The occasion is Flanders's annual dinner party, and the host is his usual self, dominating the scene with his self-importance. The topic is Lizzie and her family. Brace manages, however, to make many points in the give-and-take of the bantering.

"Why Paul," his wife managed in the tones designed to quiet a child, "you knew all this—everyone knows it."

"I don't," said Henry.

"Unlawful motherhood, I believe," Strawbridge cheerfully explained. "You Hawthornians will quite understand. I only regret that there is no scarlet letter on the bosom—no visible one. It would be very picturesque."

"It is not a jest," Mrs. Dudley said. "There are crimes we do not tolerate; there are fortunately laws and punishment—"

"Perhaps," Henry broke in, "we should set up the gallows again on the nearest hill."

"I beg your pardon?"

"As Mr. Strawbridge says, public crucifixion would be both effective and picturesque."

Cecily leaped up noisily. "Poor Lizzie," she cried, smiling hard. "I'm on her side. After all, I'm a woman too—there are times when we ought to stick together. Won't anybody have more salad? Greg will love you if you do."

Mrs. Dudley looked at her balefully.

No one had more salad.

"The brother's name is Albert, you know," Greg said. "He took my American Literature last year and described himself as a transcendental geologist. It was somewhat alarming."

"So repressed," Mrs. Meyer said. "He shovels our driveway without the slightest expression."

"And at the end," Greg went on, "he wrote me a note, a postscript to the examination. It was very seriously respectful, and commended my learning, as he called it—" Greg made the word laughable. "But he went on to deplore my failure to understand Thoreau; he was afraid I was limited by intellectual mechanism—"

"What a wonderful phrase," Cecily cried as she bustled about with dishes.

Greg smiled with a sort of glitter. "The poor chap lives in a dream, you know. Sooner or later it will collapse, and that will be the end of him."

"I don't think it's quite safe," Miss Markham whispered. "You can see he isn't normal."

"He is deplorably brilliant," Strawbridge said. "He gets nothing but A's."

"Well, there," Cecily called, backing in with a small mountain range of chocolate icebox cake and whipped cream. "I'm so glad there's something good to be said about him. I always suspected that Gardiner had a kind heart."

The laughter as she set the dish in front of her place made her glance up. Spots of color showed in her cheeks. She went back for the plates. "I think you're all too damned cynical," she cried sharply. She seized the plates, turned with an awkward lurch, tripped on an edge of the rug, righted herself, and got the plates safely to the table. She stood a moment with head bowed and the back of her right hand pressed to her brow. Everyone stared at the mountain of the dessert. (p. 47)

What is going on at the Flanders dinner party is what goes on at any faculty party, one realizes, anywhere. Gossip reigns, dominated by ostentatious allusions on the part of those who would impress their colleagues and their wives. But Brace's rendering of this party is not primarily satiric. The scene quoted above is the climax of the chapter. It is intended to show the ordinariness of people in the context of the fashionable thought at a formal gathering. On at least two occasions (earlier in the scene than the quoted passage) Cecily, Greg Flanders's wife, has stumbled, in her waiting upon her guests; her faux pas have come just at the moment when her husband or Mrs. Dudley has uttered essentially unkind remarks or made an ostentatious gesture. Cecily Flanders does not figure largely in the book. This is her only appearance. Her nervous mannerisms as well as her concern for the character of Lizzie Houghton convey to the reader that even in the world that Greg Flanders has cultivated for himself, with its high-sounding cultural tone, there is always the more human side. He does not appear to have a relationship with his wife that is a very successful one.

Other ironies may be pointed out. Albert Houghton's comment that Flanders was limited in his understanding of Thoreau through "intellectual mechanism" was probably coming near the truth despite Albert's own deficiencies. The whole segment cited from chapter eight also serves to advance the main plot by introducing various reactions to Lizzie Houghton. Henry Gaunt at this time is becoming interested in Lizzie and is curious to know more about whatever it is that the community may be thinking about her. This sampling of Brace's style from his treatment of a few characters at Flanders's party is representative of the pungent observation that accompanies the dialogue and action in the rest of the novel.

As critic, Gerald Brace assesses Anthony Trollope very highly among English writers. In his introductory essay to Trollope's *The Last Chronicle of Barset,* Brace finds that one has to go to Chaucer and to Shakespeare to find proper comparisons in this

nineteenth-century novelist (p. xv),[2] and Brace's admiration of
Trollope can be found in many other remarks made throughout
his career. One is prompted, therefore, to consider how the
writing of Trollope may have influenced the American novelist
in his own work.

First of all, some parallels and contrasts may be drawn in the
general pattern of the lives and writing habits of the two writers,
to set a backdrop for the comparison to be drawn. Trollope
assiduously worked his way to the forefront of English novelists
of his own day by prescribing for himself a regimen of early
morning rising and by setting a quota of words during his three
hour stint. Such work habits when they became known to his
fellow writers and critics caused them to denigrate the art of the
novelist. Trollope continued his work as a very able post office
official with the British Government during the same period that
he was very productive as a storyteller. As his career prospered
he gave ample attention to riding horseback and to hunting. His
novels reflect certainly these special interests. All biographies of
Trollope cite, of course, his very difficult boyhood. As C. P. Snow
says at the outset of his recent book on Trollope, "All through his
childhood and youth Anthony Trollope was more loving than
loved. Somewhere deep in his nature—this—what shall we call
it? longing? deprivation?—lasted all his life. It may have been
innate, one of the unfortunate gifts of fate, like his short sight or
his heavy lumbering physique." Snow labels Trollope's father's
plight in his forties as "a state of schizoid paranoia."[3]

Gerald Brace, although raised like Trollope to be a young
gentleman, encountered no such difficult circumstances either as
a young boy or during his adolescence, if we accept his
assurances from his autobiography, *Days That Were,* and there is
no reason we should not. Similarly we may compare Brace's long
academic career, where he was very successful in reaching his
students and carrying out the numerous other duties incumbent
upon him. The file of correspondence between editor George
Brockway and novelist Brace gives ample testimony to the fact
that Brace pursued a regimen similar to Trollope's early morning
rising and faithful adherence to a definite time schedule. "I don't
know about the results, but the effort is heroic. I fight my way
out of bed at six, get into old clothes, come down to an ice cold
kitchen, build fires, cook oatmeal and coffee, then put on two
sweaters and an overcoat, stick my feet in the oven, and try to

write."[4] It is equally true that Brace considered his avocation of sailing something that could not be interfered with for love nor money. Mountain-climbing, skiing, and other sporting pursuits also claimed a share of his time.

Obviously these general comparisons are at best curious ones. But Brace's very great admiration for Trollope may have drawn him towards certain novelistic methods that may be worth noting.

III   *Brace's Views on Trollope*

In his introduction to *The Last Chronicle of Barset* Brace takes up some of the critical points made about Trollope by Henry James and more recently by Walter Allen. James essentially admired Trollope but took something away from his praise by hints about Trollope's heavy-handedness and the commonality of his style. Similarly Brace faults Walter Allen for his downgrading that places Trollope behind Thackeray, Fielding, and Jane Austen, giving him this inferior position among the prominent English novelists for much the same reasons that Henry James had suggested (p. viii). Brace's defense of Trollope brings out some qualities in that writer that are interesting, to say the least, in an assessment of Brace's own fiction.

Brace points out that Trollope "has earned the right to be considered in a class by himself," as all writers have. He points to Trollope's "fertility of invention" which he feels is unmatched by any competitor. It is "the life-giving freshness which runs through the whole creation," not merely the fact of the abundance of the English life that is caught in his fiction (p. viii–ix). This vitality—from the early Irish novels to such very late ones as *Mr. Scarborough's Family*—is a truly remarkable achievement. One may say, by the same token, of Brace's fiction that he too has a staying power. In the later novels of Brace there is a continuing richness of texture. *Bell's Landing* (1955), *Winter's Solstice* (1960), and *The Department* (1968) are unusual in this respect. Generally speaking it is the reverse with most novelists. Our classic novelists, including Hawthorne, Cooper, Twain, and many others, have tended toward lesser achievement in the later phases of their careers.

Plotting is another area in which Trollope's critics have been pejorative. Brace distinguishes in Trollope between what critics may perceive to be casualness but what is really, underneath, true professional skill. "The great thing about his manipulation of material is that he can maintain forty or fifty characters, as he does in *The Last Chronicle of Barset*, in a state of living suspension, as it were, yet with such vitality and relevance that we believe in them and follow them from moment to moment and share their destinies" (p. ix). Brace, too, has been criticized from time to time by reviewers and editors for what is considered a weakness in plot structure in his novels. *The Spire* may be used as an example. To some it may appear that Henry Gaunt's coming to Wyndham and his involvement in the college society do not offer enough action in the sense of plot complication. It may be easy for the reader to predict the outcome of Henry's relationship with Lizzie Houghton and so forth. Yet, if Brace is viewed in relation to Anthony Trollope, then novels like *The Spire* can be seen in a truer light. "Balance, clarity, and candor" are some of the main Trollopian virtues, according to Brace's evaluation. These are qualities that one comes across in many of Brace's novels as well. "Honesty" is another hallmark that Brace cites in his overview of Trollope's fiction. "Ordinarily it might be said that one who favors honesty is in the same category as the clergyman who opposes sin, but with Trollope the evidence is that he strongly and deliberately meant it." Brace cites Trollope's *Autobiography* as the most "nakedly honest" book of its kind (p. x). One can only add, after reading Brace's *Days That Were*, that he must have had Trollope's book in mind as a guide for the tone of utter frankness that reigns in Brace's account of his growing up. In fiction "honesty" relates to quality of style and dramatic scene. Brace quotes a passage from *The Last Chronicle of Barset* to illustrate what he means by Trollope's dramatic honesty. Mr. Crawley, the poor, morally suspect and yet prideful and confused cleric is on the verge of utter defeat. Yet he rallies himself to go on with a Greek lesson (the Cyclops episode from *The Odyssey*) that he is hearing read by his daughter. Mr. Crawley draws out the tragic implications of the scene for the young girl. He compares it to the "Eyeless in Gaza" passage from Milton's *Samson Agonistes*. While this is going on Mrs. Crawley quietly comes to support her husband, putting her arms about his neck.

The point, of course, is not to try to find a comparable scene from one of Brace's novels to match with the one he cites from the masterful Trollope. It is, nevertheless, true to affirm, that in

The Spire and in much of the Brace canon one comes across scenes from the human comedy which are rendered with great fidelity to the "honest" emotional and moral responses of ordinary people whose normal predicaments after all tend to be pretty much the same from one society to another. The foibles of the academic treadmill are much the same at Wyndham as they would be at Harvard or Columbia or at Oxford. Brace evidently knows this and when he writes about Greg Flanders's stuffiness he does it in such a way as to convey to us that he is simply human. When Flanders stomps out of Henry Gaunt's office after he has failed to promote himself into the chairmanship of English we realize that his expectations have been dashed, but that he will pick up and go on his way the same as before, restoring his ego with presumably more articles on Thomas Gale, with the help of Mrs. Dudley.

Many other similarities might be pointed out between Brace's writing and the Victorian giant of fiction that he thought so well of, but enough have probably already been exampled. Trollope's well-known theme of the centrality of love as well as the unsmooth path of true love finds an echoing in Brace. Henry has no rival male vying for Lizzie's affections in *The Spire*, but the major plot line in the novel is the resolution of difficulties that impede the course of true love.

It can be said of Brace that he, too, exhibits a view of man much like the one Trollope presents. The Anthony Wyatts, Henry Gaunts, and Ralph Garretsons pursue the light of life with a fine sense of moral consciousness. Ordinary institutions civic or religious tend to play very insignificant parts, also, in the fiction of Gerald Brace. But like the novelist he admires, Brace manages to convey a sense of the individual as well as the sense of the modern society wherein the character struggles to work out his destiny. Trollope discovered his territory or world of Barchester from a single visit to the Salisbury Cathedral in southwestern Britain, with its great gothic spire and close, and its medieval streets with historic inns. Gerald Brace's New England, his fictional territory, may be discovered in and about the campus of Wyndham. The dominant image of the chapel spire above the trees should be taken ironically. Brace is keenly aware that the moral principles that were dominant in the life of those who built the church in the center of the college campus are no longer operative or conscious in the lives of a large majority. The chapel is empty; the spire remains.

CHAPTER 7

The Postwar Scene

*B*ELL*'S Landing,* Brace's seventh novel, came out in 1955. In some ways it has the sweep of a family chronicle, but not in the full sense of the *Garretson Chronicle.* The story carries us into the post–World War II era in its chronicling of New England mores. It is primarily the story of Will Redfern coming to terms with himself, with his past and with his present.

In a letter to George Brockway, the novelist commented on the mood that had surrounded the writing of *Bell's Landing:*

The book has so far been the gloomiest affair since the writing of *The Garretson Chronicle,* so the first faint stirrings of hope are very welcome. As I read your note just now it came to me that I had a dream last night; you had agreed to publish it *(Bell's Landing)* and the agreements were signed and sealed, and I was leaving (it seemed to be your office). I turned and called back in a voice no one heard or paid attention to. "But how are you going to *sell* it? No one buys novels anymore, you know." I felt the forlorn helplessness so common in dreams, and of course "you" (a dark-suited group of anonymous gentlemen representing W.W.N. & Co.) were wholly preoccupied with your executive affairs. But I hasten to add, that I'm not really feeling forlorn, not by daylight anyway, and am very happy that you like it.[1]

Bell's Landing was the name of a property on the North Shore between Salem Harbor and Manchester, Massachusetts. It was situated a little apart from the more affluent estates and near enough to the sea to stimulate the imagination of young Will Redfern and his brother Harold, who came to live there for a short period with their aunts, Evelyn and Lucy, after the market crash of 1929 when the boy's father died by suicide. The property included an early Victorian house, as well as a barn and a boathouse. In their reduced circumstances, the two boys had been living with their mother in a small apartment in Newton. Mrs. Redfern wished to establish herself as a practical nurse. She overcame some serious misgivings and allowed her sons to go to live for a period with their elderly aunts. The Redfern's grandfather, William, had been an eminent Bostonian, who gave over his business interests and dedicated himself exclusively to Boston civic and welfare activities. The boy's father in turn, had become an investment expert associated with a small firm in Boston and had lost everything in the crash. The boys had been deceived for a time about the details of William's death, a "fall" out of his Congress Street office, but his death had brought a sorrowful absorption into the lives of the young Redferns.

The novel is told in the first person by Will Redfern. His narrative is divided into four main segments: his reminiscences of that part of his youth spent at Bell's Landing; his first love affair with Sally Anthonakis; his return from World War II service in the navy and his attempt to reconcile with Sally; and finally his inheritance of Bell's Landing and his relationship to the symbolic forces of the sea but at the same time it contains more urban scenes than any previous Brace novel.

I *Boyhood Life at Bell's Landing*

In Part I Brace skillfully builds the background for his story via Will's reminiscences of his life with his two aunts. What comes through strongly is the lure of the sea. "Thalassa! Thalassa!" had been the father's cry. He was essentially a poseur, one who toyed with ship models against the protestations of his wife; but for the two boys, later, "the great thing was the sea. All of our ventures ended there, at the edge of the beach or the cliffs, where the inland world vanished behind us and we stared seeing ships and islands and the moving water, and hearing the long rush of waves curling slantwise up the beach and splashing on the rocks with a fling of white spray," (p. 43).[2]

Aunt Lucy is the slightly older of the two aunts. She loves the social scene; she is the reservoir of all things cultural; she reads the *Manchester Guardian* and *The London Spectator*. Every day for her is directed toward some beautiful experience. She reads Robert Browning and Stephen Spender to the young Redferns and holds afternoon teas. Aunt Evelyn, on the other hand, is the practical one; she checks on the boy's behavior. Her voice has a didactic emphasis as she punctuates each comment with at least one word sharply stressed. Evelyn's domain is the kitchen. These two women are also in sharply reduced financial circumstances. They have had to let their maid go. Typically Lucy arms herself with words when they quarrel. She'd like to "smack" Evelyn, or if she were younger to "beat" her while Evelyn stands prepared for any possible engagement with a saucepan.

In *Bell's Landing* time is the chief adversary:

Time had made the whole place mellow and a little untidy. There were no edges and corners. Shrubs grew wild. Weeds made a green mat in the gravel drive. Perennial flowers flourished all over the place, lovingly and unsystematically tended by Aunt Evelyn. At this time, in June of 1930, the forces had almost achieved an equilibrium, though wildness and disintegration were slowly were very slowly waxing (p. 42).

The novelist uses the contrasting roles of the two women to help establish also the large differences in the characters of the two brothers. Will tinkers, fixes the toilet, wants to get some paint to fix up the small boat, and makes friends with the Irish gardener and handyman who lives in a room in the Redfern barn. Harold is slightly older and has more intellectual pursuits. Customarily in Brace this dichotomy heralds a conflict. There is little in Part I of the narrative to endear one to Harold. He, of course, delights Aunt Lucy when he announces that he expects to read from the family library as his chief diversion at their home. We are being prepared for his eventual role as the quite snobbish and avant-gardish poet of the later story. James, the Irish-Catholic gardener, "always seemed to smile . . . but I found in time that it wasn't a smile at all . . . the open mouth really expressed life-long anxiety; it was a grimace of the deepest concern and expectation of trouble."

Book I closes on a note of tension when Will's mother returns at the end of the summer to pick up the boys and return to Hartford, where she was now employed. She viewed Bell's Landing as a place of dangerous illusions. Both Harold and Will especially are reluctant to leave and the aunt's arguments are ineffectual against the mother's concern for their proper schooling elsewhere. But Will Redfern's remembrance of the haunting sea sounds, now menacing, now sad, become an inheritance; he keeps their echoing resonances deep inside him.

II *Sally*

In Part II we learn of the fortunes of the Redfern family after a passage of about fourteen years, during which they had lived in a succession of smaller New England cities. Harold with his mother's help has managed to get into an important prep school and after that, with a scholarship, into Harvard, where he has assumed the role of a "brilliant and successful poseur" in Will's estimate. (Harold's characterization seems to be drawn at least in part from John Marquand's Allen Southby in the novel *Wickford Point* [1939], although Harold does not enter so prominently into *Bell's Landing* as does the equally distasteful Southby into Marquand's novel.) Harold is not so much a fully developed character as a foil for his brother Will, who pursues his education through his associations with friends, notably Pop Sardis and Pop's daughter's family, the Athanakis, who live in Springfield.

Pop Sardis is an old Cretan gentleman whom Will meets when he becomes an automobile mechanic. He is doggedly honest in his convictions and a type of highly thoughtful character that Brace's readers encounter in the later novels. His brand of philosophy Pop calls "logical realism." Pop considers that human unhappiness derives chiefly from men letting their desires take precedence over actuality—and also from man's refusal of nature. Pop is a reader of Bernard Shaw among others. Perhaps he sees Will as a kind of Henry Straker in *Man and Superman*— an emerging type in our technological age. He tells Will that he should work toward becoming a perfect expert—something more than the cog; he must become a creator. Will listens carefully, but does not seem swayed by this sort of thinking.

It is Pop's grandaughter, Sally Athanakis, who becomes the largest influence upon Will's whole life. Pop lived in the same tenement building with his married daughter and her three dark-haired teenage girls. Anna, the eldest, assumed the leadership role. Althea and Sally used to stare at Will with their large dark eyes. They were brought up, as Pop told Will, after the ways of the old country; they were kept in "a state of mindless virginity." Pop himself was somewhat ambivalent about the role of sex in life. He encouraged companionship between Will and Sally (whom he loved the most), yet he carefully tried

to guard his grandaughter's activities. He theorized in this
manner about sex: the world had "achieved two colossal
failures": war and sex. War might be explained in some sort of
rational way but our ideas about sex were right out of the witch
doctor's code. Will is somewhat surprised at the views of Pop,
who keeps the notions from his family. Pop would have a female
judged on her qualities—her kindness, her courage, her intelligence—but as for her virginity, it is of no concern whatever,
morally speaking.

Will secretly admires Sally, a high-school junior, and begins to
fall in love with her. She seems to have an inner existence of her
own even though the Athanakis girls do not go out much and go
together when they do. Will's friendship with their grandfather
gives him a preferred position. Sally reads Sappho and Housman
as well as other poets and plays the violin. When Will begins to
take Althea and Sally for rides in the countryside, Mr. Athanakis
is worried.

Will's brother Harold, ready to enter Harvard, makes a sharp
break from his mother over his spending habits, signaling an end
to his family commitment. Will supports his mother in this
situation. He decides to follow her suggestion of enrolling at
Kingstown Technological Institute. Will pursues his natural bent
under the direction of Mr. Chadd and becomes "an incorrigible
gadgeteer, a manipulator of and inventor of small marvels." He
returns from school to find Sally Athanakis in rebellion against
her family's sexual code. She begins to seek out situations that
could lead to trouble. Will and his mother come across Sally
hitchhiking, with three suspicious looking young men. Will
begins to contrive ways and means of meeting Sally secretly. He
is captivated completely by her vitality, her spiritual self. Sally
accepts Will's attentions but without too much responsiveness.
She accepts the idea of a passionate relationship between them,
but says she does not love him—yet. When and if the time comes,
she would never want to be afraid of it or be false in the face of
it. Will is nineteen; Sally, seventeen.

The consummation comes a year later in the spring when they
drive into the hills of western Massachusetts. Sally leads Will
without his being very aware of her intentions. The ride is Sally's
idea. She takes him to a secluded wooded area and asks him to
make love. Both are inexperienced, virginal. Will reflects on the
beginning of his affair, which has large consequences for him:

This is the place to stop, I suppose, but some of what followed was funny and in spite of our resolution not to be worried was very embarassing. Yet from the start Sally had a genius for it, and made even our mistakes and my inadequacy seem natural, and above all she made the thing sweetly and freely happy and at times full of ecstasy. We kept at it long enough to find out. (p. 142)

Both Will and Sally have a serious reaction to their sexual adventure. Their new relationship turns upon Will's desire for marriage. Sally confides their experience to her grandfather and promises him not to become further involved; Will is urged by his mother with similar advice. But Will's desires continue to be heightened. Part II closes with a separation scene. Their love-making at this point is not successful mainly because of Will's insistence.

III   *Postwar*

Will Redfern enters the navy and spends four years, mostly in the Pacific theater of war. When he returns to Boston he finds his brother Harold the leader of a new poetry movement called The Cryptics. For Will "it seemed to be a complicated series of puns." Harold's group is centered at Harvard. Harold had become a "citizen of Harvard" and for a while Will lives in Harold's suite of rooms. Will's contribution to The Cryptics was to remove a buzz in the record player they used. The Cryptics were passionate about music but in a technical way. Will thought the buzz didn't effect very much the music that went with the poetry; rather it seemed to go nicely with some of it.

As he rides in early morning from the North Station to Bell's Landing, on the North Shore, Will finds his old illusions about the place being dispelled. The heavy industrialization is an emblem for him of the loss of human hope; only the desperation of the struggle for survival seems present.

At Bell's Landing, Evelyn is shrunken and deaf and hardly recognizes Will; Lucy is withdrawn from her usual social pursuits. There is still a spark of belligerence left between the two whose economic situation has much worsened. They live on a marginal diet, surviving chiefly on James's supply of vegetables and eggs. Harold has abandoned them to their makeshift life. James has barricaded himself as best he can from the cold by stuffing oddments of cloth against the walls of his room in the barn. He tells Will of the fits of temper that Lucy sometimes had, of her throwing the phone. Will tries to shore up their life and gives them what money he can spare.

With his 1939 coupe Will hunts for Pop Sardis and learns that Sally has married a young, impoverished writer, Saul Julian, who goes from college to college, marginally subsisting in the hope of gaining some recognition from his writing. Will takes a job at Mr. Chadd's Institute until he can become reacclimated. His thoughts keep returning to Sally; he visits the Julians in their three shabby rooms. Julian appears to be a Sartrean man: "He looked like a persecuted adolescent, full of sullen misery, but his voice came out with a baritone energy and a kind of sneering competence."

Sally was still Sally. She had written during the war. For Will she was now "a grown woman more beautiful than all the queens of the Nile . . . the dark steady eyes and the warm mouth and the hair, and I knew as sure as truth that all that loveliness in her face and body was the true emblem of her inner being (p. 198). His desire for Sally had only grown stronger in the interval.

Pop Sardis's interests had turned to Darwin's *Descent of Man;* the sorrowful old man finds it "the only true divinity." From his readings he finds devotion, humility, and integrity. Pop's new synthesis comes to this: "The mind . . . makes everything into poles, like north and south, or positive and negative, but as far as he could see the one great aim of man and nature was to have it both ways. The bondage and freedom occurred together in an impossible union. Man ran from his soul in order to find it; he left home to seek a home. He reserved to himself the benefits of all extremes" (p. 201). Pop buttresses his philosophy with a recital of an old tale of Crete about a boy named Val who meets with Amaryllis, whose hair is like ripe wheat. After marrying they spent a beautiful night together, but the next morning Amaryllis was a stranger to him. Will thinks it is a sad story, but Pop maintains it isn't necessarily sad. He concludes that Will may find a girl with golden hair like ripe wheat. Not long after this interlude, Will goes to Bell's Landing to cut some wood for his aunts and meets his cousin, Jane Safford, and her daughter Betsy with blue eyes and flaxen hair.

Will goes once again to Sally and finds her husband absent. He confesses his deep love for her and asks if she is happy with Saul.

She admits her music is her primary love and the reason she left home; she and Saul had found each other necessary. She refuses Will's advances, but does not ask that he stay away from her.

IV   *A New Life—Betsy*

In the final segment of the novel, Will returns frequently on weekends to Bell's Landing, after the death of James. His new acquaintance, Betsy, assists him at times. She works well with Will on anything that has to be done. "I could see no dark corners of fear in her, no bad dreams, no shifts of vanity and deception, no color of passion. As a companion she was like a trained angel of some sort, with more sharpness of wit than most angels. . . ." Betsy, like his mother, would prefer to see Will at MIT, where he could advance himself.

There is a chance encounter with Sally again when she and her husband show up as guests at Harold Redfern's Harvard quarters. Sally now has a menial job at Filene's in order to support Saul. She became interested in Harold Redfern's poetry. Will seizes an opportunity to drive with Sally to Bell's Landing and renews his profession of love. They find Evelyn in distress. Aunt Lucy has just passed away, hours before. Aunt Evelyn does not survive the shock, dying hours later. That evening Will and Sally with the sound of the sea reminding them, as Sally said, of surrender, "slept together, holding out against time and change—until I awoke slowly to a strange bright room with a wash of rosy light on the wall. . . . Sally had gone, her clothes were gone—she had never, it suddenly seemed, been there at all" (p. 282).

Will inherits the property and lives for a few weeks with his mother at Bell's Landing. Mrs. Redfern urges Will to sell. Will wants to paint and patch up the place. Inevitably he seeks out Sally again, finding her in a slum tenement in Boston. Her husband is giving her less and less attention. He wishes to go to Mexico since his bid to enter Harvard fails. Sally admits to Will that Harold now wants her as his mistress, but that she will go to Mexico with her husband. Holding out briefly, Will finally decides to sell the place and begin a program of studies at MIT.

The closing scene is a sharing of confidence between Will and Betsy Safford. It can be interpreted as a note of hopefulness, at least; Will's request is: "Just stand by me . . . you know what I mean—don't be perverse about it." He is saying good-bye to

Bell's Landing, to the kind of life that it meant to him, to his past. Betsy agrees to stand by.

Bell's Landing is perhaps the most carefully structured of Brace's novels, if we speak in terms of the correlation of its imagery and its resonances. To begin with the opening section is effectively managed to evoke beautifully the image of the sea. The sea sounds envelop and enchant the boyhood of Will Redfern, especially, immersed as he is in the cloudedness after his father's suicide. The names of famous sailing crafts echo in his boyhood memory; "The Lapwing," "The Kestrel," and the "Kittiwake" are elicited as forms of the lovely past. They continue in the mind and the memory of Will Redfern much as the birdsongs echoed in the heart of Walt Whitman remembering his long Island experience which brought both the prospects of life and of death for the young boy setting out to be a poet. Will Redfern is drawn to the possibilities of life offered to his youthful imagination by the sights and sounds of the old house at Bell's Landing. It is the pervasive presence of the sea that punctuates each moment of life there. The sea envelops life at Bell's Landing, but the place was at times a Sherwood forest— with a clear brook running through it. For the aunts and for James the place remains the Bell's Landing of their prime. Will's *emblem* (a word used frequently) of Aunt Lucy's vision—the country of mind that she lived in—was "a big framed photograph of a Yosemite scene, with waterfall and mountain peaks, and to me it was as remote and fabulous as the moon; but father said he had been there, had stood on that very rock above the spray, and some day of course we would too. Aunt Lucy's vision was like that, and I began to think of it as having some far-off existence."

The gaunt face of James, who recognizes that the ground about the Landing is too dry for any real growth, is also a reflector of the historical moment of the thirties in America when Will was a boy.

V   *The Moral Universe*

The main forces that Will encounters later, in Book Two are social in nature: he must come to terms with his family and with women—i.e., Sally Athanakis. To replace the equilibrium of natural forces around Bell's Landing, there is now a search for an equilibrium in Will's intellectual and emotional life. His counselor, Pop Sardis, sees the Redferns in a "state of transition between old ways and new." Will struggles within himself to find "the new realities." Pop holds up Will Redfern as an example of emancipation for his daughters—Will Redfern, the young man of the present. And since we are in the age of the machine, Will must not be a mere mechanic, he must be a creator of new machines. He must be in control of the forces that go to shape his existence.

Will's initiation into sex by way of his involvement with Sally Athanakis must be considered then in the light of Pop Sardis's views. Pop believes in freedom from the taboo of sexual morality; Sally's thinking is quite the same. Will is caught in the natural desire for the expression of love in sex, and he eventually fulfills this desire with Sally in the woodland tryst. But Pop's philosophy doesn't seem of much value to Will after his intimacy with Sally. He desires more sexual fulfillment. He wishes to marry Sally. The basic tensions of the remainder of the novel are concerned with Will's attempt to resolve his relationship with Sally. Let it be said in favor of Brace that he is here positing a basically moral question in a very human manner. Brace would appear to be saying that Will Redfern's desire for Sally Athanakis is somehow wrong for him because it disorders his existence. Sally sets up in his mind a dangerous ideal, just as the sea about Bell's Landing had done. Perhaps, after all, what Pop Sardis said was true: "It might be that to make a success of love you must first renounce it."

Will Redfern in his need to understand the universe may be compared to Saul Bellow's more famous hero, Augie March. Augie's upbringing was a far more haphazard one than Will's. Einhorn initiates Augie into a career of sexual promiscuousness. But Augie, we know, always returns after his amorous adventures and their disappointments to what he calls the Axial Lines, or what may be interpreted as the moral given in a universe of experience. It is essential to remember that there *are* Axial Lines. One may say that Augie learns what every young man and woman must learn: that truly human beings are responsible beings, that one truly human does not subdue another human's nature to one's own, and that the sowing of wild oats has a certain kind of moral price tag. Perhaps that is what Will Redfern, a person much more inhibited by his heritage than Augie, also finds out.

It should be pointed out that Sally Athanakis, also, becomes acquainted with moral accountability. She is a figure of haunting beauty with her dark eyes and dark hair. Her intellectual and artistic inclinations are genuine; they remain with her throughout. It is Sally on the last evening at Bell's Landing who confesses to Will just before they go to bed that he means more to her than anyone else. Together with her grandfather, Will still is "my strength and my help in time of trouble and I guess my faith." As they begin their final love-making, it is Sally who feels impelled to experience all. "I want to *know*," were her words as the two leave behind Will's dead aunt and ascend to the bedroom on the third floor with the windows that opened upon the sea. Sally had not known the kind of pastoral vision that had been Will's at Bell's Landing. Now she comes to be identified largely with it and with all the deepest illusions of his life. But, it is important to note, Sally does adhere to her marriage to Saul. She will leave for Mexico with him simply out of sense of obligation. Her surrender to Will and to the lure of the sea has been temporary.

Pop Sardis remains for Will, however, a person whose ideas are important. His words reverberate with Will. When Will is trying to decide what to do with the house, i.e., with his own future, Pop Sardis supplies the prevailing metaphor: life is a suspension bridge, its wires and steel in a state of tension and balance. Any one force, whether it be love or freedom "or even virtue," is related to the rest. One needs a focal point like Augie March's axial lines. Will, in Pop's view, is Everyman; he is at the center of the bridge's stress and strain. He has tried to escape family. He has tried to become a Robinson Crusoe mustering his resources. He has tried to stake all on his love for Sally, but that has not availed. Pop's last advice to Will is that he simply try to live up to his talents. It seems an appropriately classical conception coming from the old Greek. Nothing too much.

Therefore, Will's decision to go to MIT is in keeping with Pop's wisdom. Perhaps his slightly hesitant attitude toward any new commitment with Betsy springs from this new realization, too. It is a beginning of a new life—one to be fashioned more after the dictates of reasonableness and equilibrium. This may sound moralistic. The plain truth is that *Bell's Landing* is not that at all.

Both Sally and Will are products of their past. They are trying to break loose from it: perhaps neither altogether succeeds in the course of the story but the close of the story points towards Will's realization of his limitations. Betsy's thoughts echo in his mind: "You have to subdue yourself for a good end." Sally had spoken these ideas when she and Will had worked together to open up Sally's summer place at Edgartown. Will at that time had repaired the boiler miraculously, it seemed to Sally, because of his patience. Now Betsy, after giving Will her promise of standing by, says: "It has to work two ways you know, I mean the standing by and the doing and the subduing and all." The new direction at least is a clear one. Balance and restraint are the goals. Perhaps these can restore an inner peace for Will Redfern. In his next novel Brace tries to show in the life of Ben Carrick how peacefulness might be maintained for a lifetime (or at least how it might have been done one hundred years ago).

CHAPTER 8

Looking Backward

A T AGE eighty-two Ben Carrick, up at five o'clock each morning, alone in his cottage that had a view of the cove where he grew up in Penobscot Bay, writes down the story of his coming to manhood, not expecting that he will ever share his thoughts with many readers. Nevertheless he feels he must give testimony to what life was like eighty years ago on the Maine coast.

Ben's narrative becomes an idyll of a by-gone period. His story is not one of a suspenseful sea-faring or the dazzle of a costume romance. It does give a remarkable insight into the life of ordinary Maine folk in the nineteenth century. Ben is primarily self-taught; his reading is an important ally for him in his old age. He begins his story by reflecting on the New World explorers. Probably many men of different nations "discovered" Weymouth Island where Ben was born, but it was George Weymouth who named it in 1605 and, since it was Pentecost Sunday, Weymouth named the north point of the Island Pentecost Point. Carrick's Cove was named after Ben's great-uncle. Ben's father and grandfather had fished out of the same waters, dug clams from the same mud and raised potatoes from the same field nearby. For Ben, Washington, D.C., and Augusta were "other countries." The age of exploration itself seemed "the beginning of time."

In recording some of the earlier incidents of his life, Ben feels as if a supernatural power, the Pentecostal Spirit, dwelt about him. He recounts how the million little herring swarmed around his father's boat and how, especially, the time he fell out of the peapod in with all the herring, he instinctively reached and saved himself by holding on to the nose of the boat—at first too clumsily grasping it—until he desperately learned not to grab too hard. That was true also when it came to his father's anxious efforts to reach out and pull him in. One had to cooperate—not panic. Or, again, when swimming in a small cove inside Pentecost Point, the naked boys "felt good all right and pretty much clean inside. . . . When we came out of the woods and saw the pastures and movings and boats in the cove it was like coming back into life all over again and making a new start."

I *Eagle*

Ben Carrick's life is lived out on the principle that a man must pretend at least that he is responsible for the things that happen to him. He must take charge of his own affairs. Ben's father, Dan, chalked up too many things to good or bad luck; and one teacher Ben knew later argued that no man was truly responsible for his actions. Like Huckleberry Finn (and perhaps like any boy who ever lived), Ben resisted schooling as much as he could; his dreams got entangled with boats. One especially preoccupied his mind. It was a half-built sloop begun by his grandfather, Andrew. Even for his grandfather the sloop must have been a luxury. It was the era of the famous Maine sloops built in nearby Friendship by Wilber Morse. Andrew Carrick had created a half-model which Ben finds on a shelf in the boathouse loft. Eventually he takes it to Iz Stanley, the boat-builder, who says it was a good one, a twenty-eight footer. The sloop itself lay only half planked and had suffered quite a bit from exposure to the elements. Ben was fifteen when Iz Stanley refused Dan Carrick's offer for it. Ben's life from then on centers around rebuilding his grandfather's sloop.

Dan Carrick is a hindrance to his son's ambition. His Pa is so self-absorbed that he is hardly aware of the boy's purpose. Nor does he act differently toward his wife and the other children; Willis is two years younger than Ben, and Vida, slightly younger than Will. Dan's saws are impossibly dull; Ben learns from a neighbor how to sharpen them by himself. He struggles with his father who appropriates for himself the piece of prime planking that Ben had diligently secured and laid out for the sloop. He learns that a good workman must learn how "to rig things so he can work easy."

When his son reaches sixteen and the sloop is starting to take shape, Ben's passion for the sloop collides with Dan's ideas about further schooling. Ben's objections result in a sudden belt on the side of the head and it starts a scuffle. Dan arms himself with a birch stick from the kitchen woodbox, accidentally hitting his wife in the face. When things subside, Ben leaves home for a short period. He encounters the Bunkers, a family of Goose Crick folk, who represent the least desirable folk of the world of Carrick's cove in their poor and slovenly existence. Here Ben meets Molly Bunker, four years older than he and sexually experienced. Eventually Ben is horrified, overcome not so much by Molly as by "the old sour smell that goes with some houses and folks." He lights out from the Bunkers as though pursued by a pack of hounds. Back home, Ben wins his fight to leave off schooling, works around the cove and puts all the time he can on his sloop.

Ben Carrick has an appetite for hard work. He cuts a ten-inch diameter tree for a mast and works mightily to get it out of the woods and to trim it down to the proper dimensions for his craft. This and other tasks have to be done while he fends off his father's attempts to turn the craft into a schooner that might be suitable for fishing and hauling.

When the sloop is done, Ben walks along the shoreway from the work site and looks back:

It didn't seem like the old world of Carrick's Cove around me any more, but had turned into a sort of Garden of Eden, all full of wonders. The boat was like a sight of everything I could ever dream of or hope for, but it wasn't all that for any practical reason—I didn't have any special plan about using her; it was just that she was born, she was there, she was beautiful and sort of mysterious. (p. 129)[1]

The sloop is called the *Eagle*. Ben's father had whittled a bird out of a piece of cedar and mounted it unpainted on top of a flagpole. He had intended an eagle, but it looked more like a sparrow when Ben came across it years after. It reminded him of his intent to carve out himself a spread-eagle and to gold-leaf it for the stern of the sloop. Ben, too, fails to complete this plan. The night the *Eagle* is finished, he feels that he has gotten into heaven at last; he doesn't even want his evening meal.

As soon as the *Eagle* is finished, a storm drives it upon the mud flats some distance from its base. As it turns out, the mishap is mainly a reminder for Ben that he has to take responsibility for his creation. He has taken his Pa's word that the mooring was strong enough.

II   *Cora*

The second half of *The World of Carrick's Cove* is written basically around the courtship of Ben Carrick and Cora Chandler. Ben is eighteen and his horizons are extended to the visits he makes to neighboring islands where some of his relatives live. The Chandlers lived at Weston Center; Cora and Ben had played together as youngsters. He remembers her from ten years earlier as the girl who could outrun and at times even outwork any boy her own age:

I remember how freckled Cora used to be. Her face looked like a comic strip's idea of Huckleberry Finn—big splashes of red and tan on a white skin. She had almost white hair, pulled back tight and braided in two braids with elastic bands on the ends. She was tall and skinny, and you'd suppose she'd be as ungainly as a colt, but she was quick to move; she could start and run like a deer—I can still see her ahead of me across the meadow as though she was flying, her skirts and hair out straight and her feet light on the ground. (p. 169)

It is haying time when Ben pulls his sloop into Miles Chandler's mooring at Weston. Cora, who is Ben's age, and her two younger sisters are helping, since their father is away. Ben first greets Cora when she is in the hay loft fixing the rigging which pulled in the hay. Cora is trying to get down from the peak of the barn without being exposed to the gaze of Ben directly below. The two sisters are enjoying it and teasing their sister. Finally Ben gets a tall ladder and assists her. He is conscious of the change in Cora:

You can say it was the clothes and hair that did it, and maybe a little the shape of her body, but underneath all that something does happen to youngsters to change them—maybe it's just the knowledge in them, like what happened when Adam ate the apple. I could tell by looking down at her head and neck and shoulders that I'd have to be careful about her; it wouldn't do to shove her off the ladder and wrestle in the hay. . . . It was the whiteness of her, and the way she bent her head and looked down at what she was doing, kneeling on the barn floor with the light coming up into her face. And I kept thinking how separate she was, how like new. (pp. 173-74)

Ben's head becomes full of both the sloop and of Cora at the same time. Those are the happiest hours of his life; he feels he has found himself as a man in those moments when he works beside Cora with the haying.

One obstacle lies in his path, one "trouble" he called it. Howard Brackett, twenty-five, begins to pay court to Cora. They had met at the graduation dance a year before. Howard has an ally in Cora's mother, Annie. Cora is embarrassed at Howard's attentions, refusing his gifts of silk spools. Ben seeks to counter Howard's designs by getting Cora to board his sloop where the two can talk, something that came easy to neither person. Cora is an able sailor herself and is impressed with Ben's sloop. But Howard Brackett's walking out evenings with Cora and his pressing her for a decision, builds an urgency in Ben. He surprises Cora in the back meadow and asks for a showdown about Howard. When Cora lets Ben know that she really has no liking for Howard, they come to an understanding. "We hadn't the least idea of touching each other, but we could talk about anything." Cora's only objection to a marriage is the practical one concerning Ben's livelihood. This love scene ends with a playful but lively wrestling match brought on by Ben's remark that he was the stronger of the two. Each time he thought he had her pinned she would wriggle away from him and once she put a scissors squeeze on Ben that takes away his breath. The physical contest seals their new close relationship.

En route to Carrick's Cove, Ben runs into rough weather and it takes most of the vanity he had acquired right out of him. He puts into Shag Island, where Tom Bunker lived—a small island such as the other Bunkers at Goose Crick lived on. These Bunkers seem tragic to Ben since they cannot afford to send their children to the mainland to school. He couldn't help thinking that they were blood kin of Annie Chandler's. Some Bunkers in the area had won the respect of their neighbors, but not these.

Back home his father seems as misdirected as ever in his round of jobs; he even tries to take over the *Eagle* for lobster fishing, which would soon turn it into a smelly fishboat. Ben, however, has begun to have dreams of going to a shipbuilding center to learn the craft. His thoughts of marriage—about Cora and himself sailing off as partners—are vague. Events themselves begin to shape his life. Dan Carrick takes off in the *Eagle* on a salvage hunt. He rams the sloop into a rocky ledge and injures himself badly. The sloop is missing. Ben finds it later with the port side all smashed in.

Dan Carrick lives for three years, badly disabled, forced to "walk" on all fours to negotiate any distance. This time the *Eagle* is beyond repair. But Cora will not allow Ben to call off their engagement. Ben labors the three years until his father's death and goes to sea for three years. He returns to marry Cora. They remain in the region for the rest of their lives, Cora's death occuring shortly before Ben begins his narrative.

III   *The Narrator*

In *The World of Carrick's Cove* the author set himself a difficult task in maintaining the narrative voice and diction of an eighty-two-year-old man, near death, who by the circumstances of his beginning had to be largely self-taught. His writing and reading habits have been developed in the later portion of his life. But Brace's craftsmanship and inventiveness are very much at work in this story. He sustains the reader's interest in the affairs of Ben Carrick largely through the steady depiction of a concrete scene. Brace borrows from his own sure and unostentatious knowledge of seamanship, of the details of boat construction and of the rounds of experience of ordinary island life. The slowly unfolding perspective of Ben's life carries an absolute ring of authenticity to it. The idiom of the earlier period is clearly caught, not rendered with any degree of studiedness. The diction is plain as befits Ben's education. The rhythms of the novel are modulated to the leisurely pace of an old man's story, yet they are dramatized according to the internal situation called for in any particular scene of the novel.

In one passage, Ben Carrick refers to *Robinson Crusoe* as one of the few familiar books on his shelf. The linear, episodic, narrative style that Defoe makes such fine use of is a partial model, too, for Brace and for Ben Carrick. Perhaps Yankee resourcefulness works well in fashioning a literary style as well as it does in building a sloop. Brace, again like Defoe, depends heavily on concrete details, like these:

Deck planking, I figured, ought to be pine, inch and a quarter by inch and a quarter, edge-nailed. You can see how much sawing and planing that would take. I didn't think I could ever do it. I looked at those rough pine boards a dozen times. I hauled one fifteen footer down into the shop, set it up on horses, got a straight-edge and pencil and drew lines an inch and a half apart. It seemed to me I'd be sawing at that board for a week. (p. 57)

None of Brace's novels is noted for its intricacies of plot, and *The World of Carrick's Cove* is more simple in basic outline and more linear in development than any other. But the episodes are fashioned so as to reward the reader by their very plainness of style. The heart of the novel is the maturation of Ben Carrick, and the episodes are arranged to give exposure to different kinds of experiences that shaped his life. James Gray wrote:

What seems to be the artless exercise in total recall of a very old man is actually a beautifully built story with climax arching gently into climax until a fullness of meaning has been achieved in a strong unsentimental revelation of the past.[2]

IV   *The Goodness of Ben Carrick*

It is a universally agreed-upon dictum that in the art of fiction it is most difficult to create a character who is essentially a good and honest person and remains so in the course of the story. A person prone to weakness or evil is simply more dramatically appealing to the reader. If such be the case, Brace set himself an additionally difficult task in the writing of this book. Yet Ben Carrick comes across as a very plausible human being. He had little formal religious training that might account for his behavior. There is little reference to what may be considered his nominally Christian background. Ben's life might be roughly compared with Crusoe's; he strove to come to terms with his creator by coming to terms with life as he found it about Carrick's Cove. He worked at getting along with his family despite their limitations. He saw in the events that overtook him the hand of the Maker. He, above all, accepted responsibilities. His story unfolds in a quiet manly way. One comes to believe in him and that his kind of peace and contentment is plausible.

Brace ran into some discontent on his editors' part regarding the ending of the novel. One thought that it was too melancholy. Brace replied: "I thought the mood of it was about right since the old man would inevitably be melancholy, and I thought it put the whole thing in the right perspective."[3] George Brockway later wrote to the novelist: "For my part I was pleased with what you did with the first chapter and with the end. I think you were right to resist my suggestion of more conflict in the ending and find that the book as a whole stands up very well in the many readings I have given it."[4] Brace from the beginning to the end of his career as a writer was diplomatic with his publishers in matters of this sort, but he also must be characterized as having the courage of his convictions stemming from an artist's true sense of what he wanted to shape in his fiction.

Is Ben Carrick's world too good to be true? Are we to believe that there were many Ben Carricks back in the 1880s in that part of New England? The answer, I think, as Brace might give it, is negative. Ben's father was surely not so admirable a personality. We first see him losing his temper and braining his horse because the animal won't heed his commands. A short while later he strikes Ben without warning and causes another accidental injury to his wife when he turns on his son. No, Ben's development is at variance with that of his father who grew up in similar circumstances. Again Brace makes it clear that women like Mrs. Dan Carrick come to premature old age through a great lack of consideration from their men folk. They are brave and durable women with great heart, but they are victims of their society at the same time. One reads in Brace, therefore, not a *laudator temporis acti* reveling in the age of innocence, but a clear-sighted singling out in this book of the hardships, the courage and the rewards, too, of a bygone age.

CHAPTER 9

Into the Sixties

I   Winter Solstice

ONE can hardly imagine at first consideration how after *The World of Carrick's Cove* Brace might in his next novel turn so fully into the life of the present age in an urban and suburban Boston and write so directly about the hell of modern society in all its vagaries. Yet this is what Brace sets out to do in *Winter Solstice* (1960), and it is what his critics feel he has achieved in a notable fashion.

Winter Solstice may be called for convenience's sake a family chronicle novel of contemporary life. But, as readers of Brace came to expect, *Winter Solstice* was also a very shrewd reading of American mores caught in the Eustace family living in East Compton, Massachusetts. Readers of *The Garretson Chronicle* will recall the fictional town in the novel—Compton. They will remember its magnificent elms, its sunny streets and its lovely old homes. The Eustaces and their friends commute to Boston to their various employments and the given mood of the book is reinforced by the absence of any pleasant landscape. Instead we have harsh subway settings, the push and pull of downtown traffic and the general bleakness which the title of the novel suggests. One measure of the harshness that Brace desires to affirm in this novel is his exact repetition of the entire following paragraph. It appears very near the end of chapter one; it reappears in the last chapter of the novel:

"Then the long morning march up the platform, the steady shuffle of booted and rubbered feet, the grim facing forward to the city, the queer silence of separate people moving shoulder to shoulder in a kind of daily oblivion. It seemed like night still under the platform roof, and yellow lights made shirls in the misty air. Sprays of rain blew in from the side. Diesels hummed or roared aloud. No one seemed to speak or show human feeling. They marched intently with closed faces (p. 12).[1]

126

I   *The Eustace Family*

Mary Kyle Eustace, twenty-nine, single, working with a Boston public relations company as a layout editor, is the oldest of three offspring of Edwin Goodman Eustace and Josephine Starrett Eustace. Patience Starrett Eustace is the next elder daughter, a college junior in humanities; the son, Mortimer Crabb Eustace, better known as "Buzz," is the youngest child, a basketball player who wins a scholarship "on the basis of his character and all-round abilities (which did not seem to include much talent for honest endeavor)." A good part of Mary's salary goes to keep Buzz at Wyndham.

Edwin is sixty-two, an engineer manqué who bounced around Tufts College, finally graduating to drink and World War I, and the Depression. He recouped somewhat during the Second World War, but eventually lost his job when his company merged with a larger one. He is a Vermonter who likes to think that if he stayed back in Starkville, as his friend Hez Applegate advised him, things might now be different for him. Cynicism marks all of his appearances in the novel, but his views are so offered that they do have about them a jovial air nonetheless. He casts his barbs at the various TV programs and their characters, but is always faithful in watching them. Currently his employment is at Commonwealth University as an assistant to the Superintendent of Buildings and Grounds or, in Edwin's own terms, "Just a plain goddamned janitor is what he is." But he manages to get a prime parking space near the President for his large Chrysler.

Josephine is descended from a more prominent line of New Englanders in the tradition of plain living and high thinking; they included writers, college presidents. She met Edwin after she graduated from Mt. Holyoke while she was doing canteen work in World War I. She prides herself on her family's past and looks to Buzz to go on in a fine career if only he can be given a proper beginning. She is an inveterate Trollope reader, to the point where the reader wonders (aware of Brace's fondness and high esteem for that writer) if Josephine's fate in this book should not have been a kinder one. Currently she is reading *Mr. Scarborough's Family,* the late Trollope novel of trenchant scorn for the ways of the law which inhibit fairness and justice. Josephine has a fair grasp of the major Trollope novels and looks forward to those few still-to-be-read novels as "her last little reserves of hope."

Buzz Eustace was five when his older brother, Charles, fell through the ice at a neighboring pond and drowned. Another brother, Edwin, had also succumbed during a polio epidemic. Mrs. Eustace transferred her dreams to young Buzz, sure that he would become a scholar if given half a chance. The basis for this confidence was very thin and not shared by Mary Kyle Eustace, who footed the bills for this "latent intellectual." Two "B's" in two courses didn't consititute talent in Mary's eyes. Buzz has a girl friend—Lollypop. "What they both are is normal," was Mary Kyle's verdict. "What ails modern youth? Nothing. Look at Buzz and Lollypop. Normal. Healthy. Uncomplicated. Devoted to sports, comic books, hotdogs. Not a brain in their two heads."

Patience Eustace is twenty-one and "somewhat prettier in the fashion of modern girls" than her sister Mary. She is in the midst of philosophy and psychology courses at Commonwealth University and sees herself as a fully emancipated person. She is condescending to her mother and Trollope and likes to remonstrate with flourishes about her mother's ancestor-worship. Brace puts it quite succinctly as he does all of the situations that the Eustaces face. Sex, which is pervasive in the campus atmosphere, frightens her though she knows all the vocabulary of sexual behavior and speaks unhesitatingly about it in classroom discussion. She takes part in college theatricals but is not successful at acting. She even knows that she is something of a poseur in her sophistication. "She even realized it was vanity, that she enjoyed prestige and social admiration, that what she hoped for and lacked was a certain kind of sexual success. It bothered her that though the young men at first came to her naturally and even gladly, they grew uncertain and backed off and treated her with respect and a touch of fear" (p. 86).

Mary Kyle Eustace is the chief protagonist of Brace's story. She is a realist. In the bleak beginnings of the wintry day which opens the novel, she sees "Hell frozen over." As she does her morning toe touches, she counts: "Ein, zwei, drei—icky, nocky nye; nicky nocky nuss—duss, bis, druss. Ein, zwei, drei—what a damn fool am I. Keeps you limber, keeps you young. Jesus." Mary Kyle can cope with her family mainly because she sees them pretty much as they are. She can give Edwin as much as he dishes out to her in sardonic humor. She doesn't allow, for example, her mother's constant echoing of Whittier's "Snowbound" to spoil her day. She reminds Edwin that his reciting of the ballad about

Sam McGee is just as nerve-wracking. Although she is supporting Buzz financially, she doesn't let that fact interfere with her telling him and his friends how she feels about their crude behavior at times. With her sister Patience she ironically is the patient one, knowing that young girls must somehow get through the college phase, outgrow it. She appears to be a very capable person at the advertising firm; she does not allow her work there to intrude otherwise upon her life.

The love life of Mary Kyle is the main focus of interest. She had been in love, once, in her senior college year with Harry Fitts, "a melancholy jester, a charming cynic, doomed to fail in any serious endeavor"; she would have married him anyway if he had not suddenly left her, telling her he could not marry any such good person as she was. Mary herself felt it was her possessiveness that had caused the split.

Several men are now interested in her. The chief suitor is Harold Chivers, thirty-five, who lives with his mother and father in South Compton. "They all three seem to live in a state of changeless and literal virtue, without experience of sin, and she had been taught that nothing could be more deadly. She eyed his profile and imagined him in the black vestments and triple-crowned hat of the Puritans. Young Goodman Chivers." Harold was most attentive to her, taking her to the better restaurants, to the latest Boston plays, conversing with her always in an intellectual vein, trying to impress her. She in turn couldn't stand his impeccable dress, his literary talk, his mathematical soul. Yet she continues to treat him civilly, giving him no encouragement whatsoever.

John Rossiter, who lives just a few blocks away with his wife and two children, capitvates her. She sings in the choir where Rossiter plays the organ and directs the singing. He always handles the group expertly; the amateurs came to make joyful sounds to make up for the lack of spirit in the religious services. John is a director with the children's aid society. His home life seems satisfactory. His wife is fairly efficient; however, she is known to be sometimes tactless and sombre. John Rossiter is as opposite to Harold Chivers as one could imagine. There is a toughness and readiness about him—his clothes, his love of sports, his common sense. He seems to thoroughly love his work and is effective in handling the trouble that the young boys provide.

In mid-February, coming home from work, as the blizzard began, Mary asks John for a ride home. The two become stranded and have to spend the night in a downtown tavern with other commuters.

It is Mary's first real chance to be near the man she secretly and hopelessly loves. She makes no effort to capitalize on her forced entrapment with John Rossiter. Rather she savors each moment of what she conceives to be a once-in-a-lifetime companionship with the man with whom she would like to share her whole being. Rossiter talks of the ills of modern society and the members of Commonwealth University's psychology department who are "committed to the dogma of sexual frustration." Rossiter's Law, as he calls it, is evoked; "The end of any train of honest thought is pure error" or, "Universal education is just a way of insuring universal misery." Mary is content just to be near him and to keep him talking. Mary regards herself also as something of a thinker. She is reading Proust, but without much enthusiasm. She wants to get to T. S. Eliot next. She has no "systematic theology," but she wants to get to know this man better, to see how he fits into the whole universe. As the evening wears on and she has to keep her head from snuggling into his shoulder, her fatigue forces her to accept that position when sleep overtakes her. As John drives her to her home, "Their eyes [take] a steady view of each other."

The blizzard brings more complications into the life of Mary Kyle and the Eustace family. Edwin, recently fired from his job at the university, has a heart seizure as, Lear-like, he confronts the blizzard's coming on. He gets out of work early, doses himself with his Old Swanee whiskey and rides the subway home, having to walk the distance from the subway station to his home. Edwin makes it to the door but there blacks out.

On that same evening Patience's life also reaches a crossroad. She has been making some progress in her attempt to get some recognition through her literary efforts. One of her poems is selected for the college magazine. And she begins to give her attentions to Anton Kedjian, who is a leading light in the university theater group as a writer of one-act plays and as a music critic. Anton is better known as Ozymandias or "Oz" by the girls. They begin to go steady. They philosophize and theologize together. She still feels opposed to those college males who were more predatory, it seems, than those primitives she studies in her courses. "But none the less she admitted to herself a profound unease, a longing for understanding, a need for the beginnings of marriage; she shared with all the others, savage or cultivated, the pervasive sexual consciousness of her surroundings. She saw Anton Kedjian as a challenge and a mystery; even his name magnetized her, and she read Omar Khayyam and had glimpses of ancient oriental worlds beyond her ken" (p. 169). Thus on the night of the big storm and a college party that kept up till dawn, "Patience and Oz lay together all night in a fiery blaze of passion."

That evening's storm also produces problems for Buzz Eustace. He is driving home with his Wyndham teammates from a game in Williamstown after a big victory. Given the icy roads, Buzz is driving too fast, goes into a spin, and strikes a stone parapet, killing Cliff Wahn seated beside him. Buzz is plunged into misery over the accident. He hardly responds to Mary Kyle's call about the father's coronary stroke. John Rossiter goes to Wyndham and urges Buzz to attend the funeral that afternoon, calling upon Conrad's *Victory* for an example of moral courage. (Buzz had read only that one, because it had the least number of pages.) Buzz forfeits the remainder of the semester's work, and gets a part-time job as a soda jerker. John Rossiter recommends the army for a couple of years.

Patience's night of love results in pregnancy. She refuses to tell Oz about her condition, not wanting his life to be impeded. Mary Kyle talks with her sister realistically but sympathetically, and both realize it is a great blow to the mother's pride of family. Mary Kyle raises the question of abortion but calls it a "bad idea." Without Patience's knowledge she seeks out Anton. He appears to her a person of intelligence, but not so awesome as Patience's descriptions. Anton rushes to see Patience when he learns about the pregnancy.

Patience's college friend Edna encourages abortion, but Patience is revolted at the idea. She can no longer face living with her dorm partners; she feels their morals are odious. When Mrs. Eustace learns the facts, she states her plan to leave the town and go to Portland with Patience to escape public attention. Meanwhile, Patience makes a suicide attempt by cutting her wrist in the bathtub, but Mary Kyle bursts in and rescues her.

At this point yet another suitor for Mary Kyle appears. He is

Tom Heath, a Commonwealth University archaeologist and a friend to Edwin Eustace, who is recovering well from his stroke—well enough to be drinking his Old Swanee. Heath seems to Mary Kyle a very well adjusted person. She sees him as "rational, realistic, objective, and unpretentious," yet she seems not to like him at first because of these very qualities. He is sympathetic with the family problems and is quietly courteous and attentive towards Mary. When their talk comes around to Christianity in the modern world, Mary's comment is that if it were intended for the weak and the helpless, it has not been adequate. "He shrugs, smiling a little." Tom Heath's only immediate family is his father who is elderly and somewhat infirm.

Patience gets over her fit of despondency but she has an early miscarriage. Mary Kyle begins to feel slowly more compassion for her. Meanwhile, John Rossiter is pushing the idea of Mary's taking a job in his Youth Center. She comes along at his request to Fenway Park to help with five girls at an afternoon's outing. Mary is curious as to John's reasons for wanting her as an assistant. Harold Chivers meanwhile makes a final desperate proposal to Mary Kyle. He cannot seem to comprehend her strong, repeated negatives. But Mary's suitors are reduced by one.

Patience and Tony are drawn together by their difficulties. Both are desirous of marriage. Mary remains Patience's best friend and confidant and helps the lovers break the news to Josephine and Edwin, a delicate diplomatic mission. Tom Heath continues his weekly visits to Mary Kyle.

In mid-May several friends of Buzz are having a loud party in the Eustace home. When Mary tries to quiet things down, she gets only smart remarks from the group. Half drunk, Buzz tries to champion his sister. Mary Kyle floors the one that had wanted to dance with her with a hard righthand slap and routs the rest of them out of the house as Josephine comes upon the scene.

Mary Kyle helps Patience arrange for her final departure from the Eustaces. Patience is aware that she will be the one to carry the practical burdens of the marriage; Tony, she realizes, is given to Platonic dreams. But she feels that they, like other young people, are seeing through the shams of society and are creating a new honesty in living. The wedding comes off without any problem with Josephine and Edwin in attendance.

Mrs. Eustace's declining health, Patience's bills and the home maintenance give Mary Kyle little time for herself; the attentions of Tom Heath and the job offer of John Rossiter continue to occupy her, too. John invites her for a long ride to an orphanage north of Concord, New Hampshire. Mary chooses the occasion to tell him it is their last ride together (as she ponders Browning's lines). She will not take the job; she will give up the chance. It is not that she loved him any less; she has to act on the matter. John does not appear to be greatly affected by these announcements. He continues to counsel Buzz about going into the service for a short period. Mary confides to an old college friend that she is getting interested in Tom Heath. Sandy Farr's advice is to grab him before it is too late. Mary Kyle looks at her friend coldly. "Just go slow, Sandy. This is my show, after all." Mary Kyle appears to be bolstered up. At the office she decides she may accept Joe Bass, the office romancer's latest idea for a dinner-dance date. On arrival home from work she discovers her mother very near death. After the funeral Mary Kyle feels death was also her only "release."

Josephine's death apparently sparks Edwin. He starts taking care of his own needs and resumes his ballad singing. The year has come round again to the winter. Mary Kyle takes up her reading. "Her life had leveled off, and the Proust carried her across an endless plain where life existed simply as an awareness, without activity or without body, yet with a curious importance. . . . She was intensely curious about Proust's world, but never for a moment part of it: the magnification of vanity and self seeking seemed like a preposterous nightmare with no end and no sane purpose. But it went especially well with a train, five days a week forever" (p. 235).

Tom Heath before departing after a summer session takes Mary Kyle for a sail off Marblehead in a rented dinghy. His self-assurance with the boat and his amiable chat make a strong impression upon her. She knows he wants to talk to her in confidence about his personal life—his father's incapacity. The beautiful outing ends with a visit to his parent. Tom's proposal follows. Actually he has been reticent about asking Mary to marry because of his increased burden. He would rather she waited and not hurry her answer. John Rossiter jogging around the block partly interrupts the proposal scene on Mary's doorstep.

The next evening John Rossiter returns to the Eustaces. He
confronts Mary with a challenge to explain her behavior to him.
She remains cool through his long recital of love for her. It began
the night of the blizzard. His relationship with his wife is one of
dutifulness and even love and respect. It would not permit him to
desert her. He demands to know if Mary Kyle loves him. "You
know it" is the answer he gets. Mary Kyle a moment later says
"yes" to his question of marriage, but asks, "How?"

"Does it matter how?" He gripped her shoulders and leaned to kiss
her. He smiled with a sudden wildness and pulled her close. She
touched his bushy hair and ran a hand down over his temple and cheek
and nose. "Will you?"
"Yes," she said.
"Now? Tonight?" He watched her with a kind of glitter. His hand
held her breast.
"You mean—tonight—or for life?"
"I mean—everything. I mean just us two, now and tomorrow."
"Leave your family? Desert them?"
"Yes!" His hands were rough and demanding. "I mean—"
"You'll cut off your arm?"
"Yes! Yes! His passion enveloped her. She couldn't draw back or
even stir. He pressed with all his strength. "I tell you, this is all there is
for me. I love you entirely, more than life itself, or the world, or
anything."
"No" she said abruptly. "No." (pp. 252–53)

When John persists in his efforts she squelches them with
force, asking him to "Stop acting like a sex-starved runt."
It is Patience's turn to try to give counsel to her older sister
about Tom Heath. Mary confesses to her sister that she would
marry readily if she really loved him and felt like going to bed
with him, but she does not, for all his fineness. She stops short of
telling her sister her passionate feeling for Rossiter. Patience's
advice, like Edna's, is to marry Heath. "I think the biggest thing
in love is friendship" is Patience's wisdom. When Tom Heath
asks again Mary Kyle says "yes." The decision, however, makes
her uneasy. She had never confided to him her real feelings for
John Rossiter. Coming out of work she sees John Rossiter near
Haymarket Square talking to a group of teenagers who seem
agitated. She waits till John talks to them and indicates he will
help rescue one of their group being held in a cellar by another

gang. Mary Kyle tells him of her decision. Hurriedly he begs her not to and leaves with the young boys. The morning paper carries the headlines about the stabbing of John Rossiter. Mary Kyle tries to make it to the hospital, but it is too late.

In the last chapter of *Winter Solstice* there is a vignette of Mary Kyle's life four months after John's death. She is now at work at the children's aid society, helping the new leader of the institution. We learn that sometime after John's death in a last meeting with Tom Heath she had told him of her passion for John Rossiter. "A sort of dramatic arrogance had flared up when it shouldn't have, she knew, and she had told her love almost with pride—or even vanity, perhaps—and had dismissed Tom Heath as one unaware of the reality of passion. Yet he had indicated he would try to understand. He would come back. He had already gone when she insisted it is over" (p. 282).

Winter Solstice thus summarized may very well sound like a TV soap opera. It does not, however, read like one. It takes a searching look at what Compton, Massachusetts is like a hundred years after Randall Garretson had lived there and it is far from a pleasant prospect.

An epigraph from Chapter 5 of Thomas Browne's *Hydrotaphia, Urn-Burial* appears before the first chapter:

Darkness and light divide the course of time, and oblivion shares with memory a great part even of our living beings; we slightly remember our felicities, and the smartest strokes of affliction leave but a short smart upon us.

The Browne quotation goes a long way toward giving us the mood of *Winter Solstice*. It suggests that its aging author (again like the older Trollope) was still looking unflinchingly upon contemporary life. Browne was closing his famous essay on the great theme of mutability. Brace's use of the passage underscores both the grimness of modern life and yet the ephemeral nature of both our suffering as well as our happier moments.

In no previous novel had Brace undertaken to give such a comprehensive view of modern existence. The Eustace family is chosen for their representativeness. As always, Brace is working with the characterization of ordinary people. It is worth noting that within the Eustace family the author is combining the rustic, small-town background of Edwin with the more urban, sophisticated, and socially prestigious background of Josephine. Their suburban family life can be taken as a microcosm of many other such families in Boston and elsewhere.

Mary Kyle Eustace is the character that Brace himself wishes to primarily delineate in this work and it is worth the while to try to come to terms with her as a kind of moral focus on human beings as Brace depicts them. By seeing the vicissitudes she faces and her attitudes as she undergoes them, we may approach more closely the values of the author himself.

There is no doubt about Mary Kyle's wit and imagination as a great ally in a world that wants to subjugate her to its own grimness. She holds an even keel, intelligently using conversation with suitors and with family to try to get to the heart of the situation.

Brace posits honest passion in his heroine, and passion spins the plot. But in Mary Kyle there is abundant evidence that passion is not the sum and substance of man's existence. The author is well aware that sexual promiscuity is increasingly the vogue of the times. One risks a considerable amount of reader appeal by going against the prevailing sexual mores and having the heroine remain a virgin when the man she has a real passion for also wants her at the same time. Mary Kyle is, of course, no prude. She had said she would marry John Rossiter. But her good sense and her virtue combine to make her withdraw her word when she sees, a moment later, that Rossiter's desire for her derives from his frustrations with his own marital situation, not from a desire to make a new life with her.

Her second major decision in the novel is also humanly presented. She is thirty and has found in Tom Heath a man whom she can marry and be reasonably happy with. It is her fundamental honesty after Rossiter's death that brings about her confession to Tom Heath that her attachment to the social worker was her primary love. Therefore, when she decides to carry on the work of the man she had secretly loved, she continues to be very honest with herself. She had borne the brunt of her family's problems; she freely chooses to spend her time continuing to help young people when they need help most desperately. It is not some vague or vain self glory that she seeks. Harold Chivers converses with Mary Kyle, and asks if she enjoys her new work:

"Enjoy?" she begins a quick reply, then pauses, "Why—I hadn't thought. It's a mess, of course, you can't imagine—" She saw his orderly face and figure and laughed again. "Yes, I enjoy it, now that you ask. It's worth going to town for—that's something, isn't it? And I feel virtuously poor, but honest. Not that I should boast at this stage of the game, but it's the kind of thing that has a good deal to look forward to. I don't believe we'll ever really get straightened out, but at least—at least." (p. 283)

Mary Kyle Eustace, then, reflects those virtues which Brace himself must find still possible and desirable in a changing world. It is clear that families such as the Eustaces are facing extraordinarily difficult times, one problem mounting upon another. One infers from the implications of *Winter Solstice,* that Brace finds no institutions in the modern community that can really cope with the crazy tempo of modern life. Meaningful church activity is reduced to choir meetings. Edwin plays a fraudulent game with his employers. Mary Kyle's job as a layout editor at the public relations firm is meaningless. While the children's aid society does try to help youngsters, that it is not highly effective is pointed up by the fact and manner of Rossiter's demise. It is, however, an honest attempt. Brace does not much involve his characters in political affairs in a direct way. The university as a force of enlightenment and common good may be said to be present as a strong community force in every novel that Brace wrote. In *Winter Solstice,* although it touches the lives of all the characters in definite ways, it seems in no real sense to be effective. At times it appears to produce more negative than positive results. One gets the feeling that its conglomeration of courses in psychology and philosophy are more detrimental to Patience Eustace than helpful. Tom Heath, however, does partially redeem this adverse image of the university. He strikes one as a very balanced person.

It cannot be fairly said, however, that Mary Kyle alone has the qualifications for sustaining life in the modern world, because Patience succeeds, too, in her trial and will fill her proper role. She is both accountable and responsible. Edwin and Josephine represent less effectual ways of coping with modern existence. Perhaps Josephine's death is an indication of the lesser durability of her more "elitist" family tree. Tough old Edwin Eustace hangs on more by virtue of his drinking and his up-country toughness than anything else. We cannot expect too much, it seems, from Buzz, but, in the light of the book's moral rhetoric, we can bet that he will somehow stumble along.

Harold Chivers's father likes to compare Mary Kyle Eustace to Boadicea, the early queen of Britain, who led a revolt against the invading Romans. She was finally defeated, but not before causing the death of 70,000 Romans and their allies when she took her own life. Brace at least seems to be saying in this story that his modern heroine is facing very difficult odds, too, and doing very well withal.

II   The Wind's Will

Four years after *Winter Solstice* Brace, at age sixty-three, returned to familiar territory, eastern Maine, for the setting of *The Wind's Will.* It is a novel with much of the somberness of the previous story, and it renders well the ambience of a small rural community, just as *Winter Solstice* had captured the ambience of metropolitan Boston. In this tenth novel Brace also was returning to the *Bildungsroman;* the essential story is of a young person coming into manhood.

He is David Wayne, high-school senior and son of the town minister Amasa Wayne, a graduate of Wyndham. David's essential struggle is with the puritan ethos which is carried to an extreme in his father. His mother, Angela, is a dutiful wife entirely subdued by the grim husband. The older brother, Simon, had left home early because of a clash with Amasa.

David has, nevertheless, thus far managed to live a stable life. He has several friends including Albertine Robichaud, his French teacher in high school; Gretta Hasbrouk, the doctor's daughter; the gang at Hardy's grocery store where he has a part-time job; and especially Doc Larrabee, the ex-Harvard man, ex–baseball player and full-time village renegade philosopher from whom the young men in South Portage seek counsel as they drink beer in his quarters across the river in Snowden.

Brace begins the novel with a well-conceived incident that shows some frustration and tension in the life of David Wayne. He is the valedictorian of his high-school class; but on graduation night he skips out of his speaking commitment. He had had a clash of views with his principal, who is backed by Mr. Wayne. The reader finds David at Doc Larrabee's trying to explain himself. Doc is an honest counselor. He tries to find the real reason behind David's behavior. Doc's allusions to philosophy are not readily assimilated by David, but Doc makes some applications to life. He tries to show him the difference between true courage and fear. He puts it in Christian terms for the young man, although he himself is "not much of a believer." But there is more than rambling fancy in Doc's views: "If you want to sleep at night you'll have to come to terms with humility." What happens in the remainder of the book is an account of how those terms are met in the life of David Wayne.

The Waynes have lived in South Portage for nine years. They are from a more rural area, so that "David's world had always been dwindling and diminishing" in the sense that the farming days were gone, the forest cut down and the mills by the streams were mostly ruins. His middle name is Percival and he had, at twelve, become ashamed of it because of his friend's taunts. Yet he read and reread the version of the Arthurian legends about the pure knight that his uncle, the English teacher from Connecticut, gave him.

David resents his father's attacks on his friend Doc as a free-thinker. The best way he can live with his father is to avoid these clashes as best he can.

David survives the graduation speech cop-out. He invites Albertine, who has become his secret object of attention, on a farewell date, since he realizes she will be leaving South Portage. Albertine has been well educated, and she knows how to have fun with her students, how to bring out the best that is in them. At the same time she is open with them on sexual matters. She is candid with David and tells him what her own love affairs have been like. It appears at times that she admires David himself. She calls herself a hedonist, yet she is in no way condescending to the townspeople, even though they are her inferiors culturally.

After some hesitation she agrees to accompany David to his old skiff for a ride down the river to Bateman's Castle, a hideout cave of the high-school boys high above the river. The two have coffee and snacks at the cave. Talk is about religion and David's father, but soon David "found his hands were against her shoulder and he was trying to kiss her." David's wildly romantic notions of love-making drive him on, but Albertine simply says no and brings him to his senses. She turns the situation around by making him see that his approaches were crude, that she, too, had a sort of vision of love, but that it was of sharing. David is further set back when a group of his pals, knowing of the date with Albertine, trail him to the cave, make catcalls from a distance as he leaves, and steal the skiff, forcing the two to walk home amidst the June black flies.

Talk gets around. David conceals from his father the real nature of his outing and promises himself he will talk about it with Doc Larrabee. He has a scrap with Art Sawyer about the skiff and briefly has the better of him. At Hardy's grocery he passes off the kidding he gets from the girls about the trip to Bateman's Castle.

With Doc Larrabee, David gets another dose of moral philosophy. Again there is more wisdom to it than what one might ordinarily expect. Doc is careful not to want to "subvert the son of a dedicated Christian." He stresses the mind's power of control, not ultimately—but in a large degree. Doc had a wife who left him, a daughter who is ashamed of him, and a son who died in the war. His dad had been a small-town newspaperman, a Cleveland Democrat. Doc's nonconformism has come from his dad. Doc likes to expound William James's notions: "Use all your faculties, body and brains, and you'll have a better time of it— use them for the common good and you'll have the best time. I don't rate very well on his scale" (p. 96).[2]

A party at Gretta Hasbrouk's gives an insight into the young folks' social milieu at South Portage. Dr. Hasbrouk is too much in attendance with his admonitions of "nothing in excess," monitoring as he serves the cake and ice cream. Mrs. Hasbrouk stays mostly in the dining room and is quite reserved. Later on the couch after the others have gone, David's desires are stirred again. Gretta, awed by rumors of Albertine and David at the cave, tries rather clumsily and fearfully to get David to become intimate. But Dr. Hasbrouk breaks up the party.

The main complication in David Wayne's existence comes with the arrival in South Portage of Mrs. Joanna Wexler. In a way she is a distinct contribution to the town with her varied cultural interests. She aids with the church affairs and is on a first-name basis with the Reverend Amasa Wayne. The word is that her family had been destroyed in Europe in the War. She had presumably married again, in Boston, but "was driven out." David begins to worry about Joanna and his father when it is rumored they are frequently together. One evening David offers to walk Joanna home from a meeting held at the Waynes. Joanna asks him in and offers to play the piano for him. David is impressed by the room, the music, the woman herself. Images of the age of Sir Percival began to stir in him. His father quizzes him anxiously about his visit to Joanna's house and about his promise to help her with house-painting. The Reverend Wayne's own interest in meetings with Joanna continue.

Shortly afterwards, David walks late one evening by Joanna's rooms. He spots his father leaving. Impulsively, he goes to her door. Joanna offers herself to David completing her seduction of him. He is somewhat ashamed and disappointed but feels compelled to pay more visits to Mrs. Wexler; he feels he is her prisoner. She grows repulsive to him, though there seems to be two Joannas: the former gracious, cultured musician and the present lustful, middle-aged woman. The affair comes to an end as abruptly as it began, with Joanna making no real attempt to prolong it.

Will Hardy, David's boss at the supermarket, is the one who concernedly tells him of the growing talk about Joanna Wexler and his father just at a time when his father's ministry is improving. Faced with his own son's accusations Amasa simply pleads guilty. He insists he was the tempter, "the chief of sinners." When David, too, confesses that he has been seeing Joanna nearly every night for the last two weeks, Amasa is momentarily shaken, but regains his characteristic prideful role. He wishes David to find Simon and deliver a message asking pardon. "I will bear all the blame I can. I don't intend to evade." Later as he drives David to the bus for Boston, Amasa says that he cannot repent; Joanna's image is before him. David also thinks about Joanna. He hopes he wouldn't ever meet her again, but "felt a strong bond with her, in spite of everything."

With fifty-five dollars in his pocket and not much of an idea where his brother Simon is except for a postcard that indicated he had been working and living in the vicinity of Fenway Park, David arrives in Boston. Hazel McCune, Albertine's roommate, is on the same bus with him; she probes him a little about his trip and then arranges to have him stay with a group of university students, to help make his money last. They are a friendly and helpful crowd, especially Steve Myers. This new world of the university makes a strong impression on David. When Steve Myers learns David had some hopes of attending the University of Maine he does all he can to counsel him, since he seems so preoccupied with his mission.

David traces his brother to a ramshackle apartment. A young woman is reluctant to speak with him. Finally she accepts David as Simon's brother. Simon has become a night watchman. In answer to David's query, Mary says, hesitantly that they are married. David finds Simon at Rocco's Tavern, off Washington Street. His brother seems stunned at first and David has to reveal in the darkness of the tavern who he is. Simon doesn't care to know anything about Amasa. He laughs at the idea of "marriage" with Mary. Simon's dream is to get some capital, go to the Florida Keys, and acquire a few fishing boats to rent. Maybe Mary can help with some of her money. Simon feels Amasa is still just an old puritan thunderer. The only concession he will make is that he'll send some money to Mrs. Wayne when his big deal goes through.

When David returns to the university rooming house, Steve Myers again helpfully talks to him about his brother. He talks about Maine and how some of the students have interesting jobs related to archeology, helping to explore glacial action on Mt. Katahdin. On the morning of his departure, Steve again unselfishly spends time encouraging David to make some decisions of his own in regard to his family. The university students and their talk brings back his conversations with Doc Larrabee. He realizes that Hazel McCune and Steve Myers had both aided him without looking for any return for themselves.

Back home he learns from his mother that Amasa has left. He has driven off in the old Plymouth with Joanna. "I leave my home, my wife and son, my life, I go forth into the unknown with the woman I love." His mother speaks candidly of her life with the Reverend Wayne. He was always a ladies' man. Her hopes are in David but she feels sorry for Amasa because she knows that he will not be able to get along with her. David resumes his job at Mr. Hardy's. He speculates that both Amasa and Joanna would die—perhaps in some kind of pact. The village gossip is plentiful at the store, but Bill Hardy is kind. Mr. Hasbrouk catches David outside the store and pointedly tells him "No more parties, no more dates, no more nothing—understand? . . . My advice to you David Wayne, is to get out of town; clear out."

The parish executive council tells Mrs. Wayne she can stay as long as the house is not needed, probably a couple of months, with a month's salary provided. Mrs. Wayne turns to David for advice. He works on lawns and gardens for additional money and makes application to Orono for student aid in the fall.

In August, Hazel McCune calls to ask if he had heard about Simon. Steve Myers read about a tavern brawl and guessed it was David's brother. A woman had stabbed Simon. David's guess that it was Mary Kaminsky proves right. He takes the bus back to Boston, staying again with Steve Myers. The university atmosphere still draws him. They talk of Doc Larrabee's ideas and of man's fate. Steve's ideas generally agree with Doc: "A man can invent a new environment for himself, I mean like a city apartment where nothing is what you call natural, but he can't invent a new man—he hasn't so far anyway" (p. 232).

Simon arrives home with "some jade stones, and a carved ivory dragon two feet long, and some Japanese swords, and an uncut yellow diamond about the size of a small olive." He does not press charges against Mary Kaminsky for the near murder; he feels simply that he had underestimated her: "she's just a basic female woman, not very smart, I admit, but with guts and self-respect" (p. 234). Simon is not much worried about his return to South Portage; he rather revels in the idea of his dramatic return. He is living up to what the town expected of its former baseball hero and prize-fighter. Angela accepts his return with resignation. Late that same evening the old Plymouth comes noisily into the back yard. Amasa has returned. Throughout the business, neither Mrs. Wayne nor Simon knew of David's own involvement with Joanna. Amasa's rumbling voice echoes in the house while Simon snores. David waits for some explosion but silence prevails the rest of the night. Angela gives Amasa some sleeping pills. In the morning, his mother tells David of Amasa's verdict about himself. "He thinks he has to die." He feels his guilt was greater than Simon's or David's. His spiritual crises brings on a five-day constipation which he will not allow Dr. Hasbrouk to treat. He allows God no options in his case. The next day he is missing again. In the evening, David spots a light in Joanna's room. She tells him she is moving to Boston but that she hasn't seen his father that day. Joanna comes to the Wayne's shortly after and confesses to David that Amasa has been to her apartment in a rage. She has told him to go jump in the river. At the water's edge David finds his father's body with a rope tied to an iron ring attached to a float. David does what he can to arrange the corpse before he runs for help.

Yet for the Waynes life goes on. They move to a small tenement. David again withstands the flow of gossip. He fills in at the baseball game with the town team on Labor Day. He provides for his mother and brother as best he can; they somehow seem to get along better than before. The novel ends on a note of hope. Judy Bligh seeks out David and asks him to accompany her to Orono for the Freshman Week activities.

The title of Brace's novel was borrowed from a refrain of Longfellow's "My Lost Youth" (1855), just as Frost had borrowed the first part of *A Boy's Will* from the same source. The Maine poet's ten stanzas were a reminiscence of his earlier days in Portland: "A boy's will is the wind's will, / And the thoughts of youth are long, long thoughts." It is not difficult to see a correspondence of mood in Brace's book to Longfellow's poem and to Robert Frost's volume, which contained a poem called "The Trial by Existence."

The Wind's Will contains the most compressed narrative of any of the novels Brace wrote, with the exception of *The Wayward Pilgrims*. The action is virtually contained in the few weeks between the high-school commencement of David Wayne and the end of July, when his father commits suicide over his involvement with Joanna. This compression puts a large onus on the novelist, especially when there is a serious moral theme to be developed and significant character delineations to be made. In this respect *The Wind's Will* may be compared to *Winter Solstice*, whose action was contained within the cycle of one year. Both fictions center on family life and its complications in the modern world. Brace seems as effective in evoking the city and its suburbs as he is with the small-town milieu, which, this time, is not a coastal town but some miles inland on a river.

R. V. Camill charges that the exchanges between father and son are incredible.[3] Actually Brace is very much in control here. David never returns to Joanna once he learns his father is actually her lover. He exhibits a feeling of wanting to help his father in his remorse. David is not voluble at all. When one talks to an Amasa Wayne, one gets a word in whenever he can between his self-dramatizings. Clearly, Brace throughout his novels never sensationalizes sexual behavior. Thus in *The Wind's Will* he is deliberately deromanticizing the situation between David and Joanna. But he is by comic-realistic touches showing the reader the honest effects of sexual behavior in the life of the young man. He is not "reading through a glass darkly," nor is his imagination without passion; rather he is looking with a clear daylight vision at what some modern novelists choose to obscure or exploit.

It is, of course, a serious misreading of the text, also, to call Doc Larrabee "a desperate old drunk." He, surely, among all the people in South Portage is the farthest removed from desperation; neither are his two or three ounces of alcohol a day anywhere near drunkenness. Brace gives Doc Larrabee an important role in the formation of young David Wayne's character—a role that he would not likely assign to a "desperate old drunk."

Both Albertine and Doc Larrabee are persons of particular importance to a full understanding of the theme of the story. David learns after Albertine's departure from the town that she and Doc were friends; they had intellectual interests in common. Albertine sends Doc a gift—a new critical work on Voltaire. Doc characterizes his own life as a holdover from the naturalistic era of the first decade of the century; he has become a "professional hermit," but his utterances are listened to carefully by David. He may not comprehend them very fully.

Albertine has told David she was a Catholic, but "perhaps not a *good* Catholic." She evidently didn't care for some of the rituals and rubrics. Doc, too, tells David that the Catholic Mass is the only place he feels comfortable, though he moves around to all the churches at least once a year. But he does feel the Catholic's "grace" is an illusion he can't really share.

In the last scene of the novel, after a long interval away from Doc, David seeks him out. Doc is currently the object of an inquiry by the town's social service board. They think him a vagrant and wish to assign him to a pauper's home. Doc thinks he can (with the help of a friend who owns a lumber yard where Doc makes his bed over the office) escape this fate. David is still thinking what it was that "possessed" his father. It was something inside him that he couldn't control. David didn't rule out the idea of devils. Doc's final advice to David (as he hands him a copy of William James) is that he "must build a will and mind of your own." The repeated references to William James's views in the book and the kind of sympathy that Brace extends to Doc's characterization lead one to believe that here, much more than in other novels, Brace is sharing his own philosophical preferences. Doc's missionary efforts have not been without fruit. We learn about a seminary student who came to him and was converted into a very successful high school teacher in Portland. Doc's parting advice to David is of the essence: "A man has to remember to think it out . . . any troubles I have are my own damned fault, I can tell you that. I fixed my life the way it is and I'm ready to take the consequences."

Brace's novel is not so satisfactory in the handling of the Boston episodes and the characterization of Simon. Simon (Peter) Wayne is apparently akin to Eugene O'Neill's famous brothers Simeon and Peter in *Desire under the Elms*. Simon Wayne leaves home much earlier, however, than did the Cabots, at age thirty-nine and thirty-seven. But, like the sons of old Ephraim, Simon Wayne has traveled far in search of gold. When David finds Simon in the Boston tavern he fills David with dazzling claims of adventure. Later, after the stabbing, when Simon is back home recuperating and sponging off his worn-out mother, his role as a character foil for David is complete.

Clearly Simon has failed. All of his experience gained from his necessary shifting for himself and from his sexual promiscuity have not provided him with any stability compared with David's from his sexual encounter with Joanna, his facing up to his family obligations and his acceptance of his father's fate. Brace is not writing off Simon as a total loss. He does learn to respect Mary Kaminsky, the woman who nearly fatally stabbed him. He will not press charges against her; he has learned a little about the nature of women. Also, it is Simon's humorous stories about nude girls that gives a few moments of lightheartedness to Mrs. Wayne. On the other hand, Simon's portrait is weak in its lack of depth and action. We never see him with his woman or as a prize-fighter, or in direct confrontation with his father. He is *potentially* an Apeneck Sweeney or perhaps one of O'Neill's Last Chance Saloon boarders, but he is not fully realized.

On the other hand, in the characterization of David the novelist handles very well the pull and magic of the big city for a young New England small-town boy. Brace has, for example, a good feel for sports, particularly baseball. He captures well the mystique and lure that Fenway Park, the home of the Boston Red Sox, has for young people like Simon and David. Fenway is the mecca for the small-town visitor to the largest New England city.

Simon, the home-town high-school baseball great, had gravitated to Boston and got a job as a maintenance worker when his father had forced him to leave home. David seeks out the baseball park, since it was the last clue he had of his brother's whereabouts.

In the episodes that concern the influence of the university environment upon David, Brace can be criticized for insufficiently building the atmosphere of the dormitory, the intelligent conversation, and the camaraderie by which David decides to continue his studies at the University of Maine. It is not that these impressions are not strong in themselves; there does not seem to be an appreciable time for their absorption into the novel in view of the large upheaval in the young David's existence.

Brace, then, in *The Wind's Will*, as Thomas Curley points out,[4] is doing something fairly extraordinary in an age that can be primarily characterized as one in which novelists do *not* write about young heroes who grow up countering the natural forces that surround them with an effort of their minds and their wills to make a moral struggle. Doc Larrabee has taught David the Conradian viewpoint that "all human beings are cowards. That's our natural condition. We overcome it sometimes, by vanity or passion or what you call will. But the common condition is fear" (p. 21). David has learned from his own experience as well as from the failure of his father and brother; he has fashioned a will of his own.

In *Winter Solstice* as well as in *The Wind's Will*, Gerald Brace continued to show an ability to present significant characters in action. Both novels also remind the reader that human responsibility remains despite the chaotic nature of our world. To maintain balance despite the chaotic scene around one becomes more and more difficult. Some of the values of the older New England heritage are still recognizable in the lives at least of some of the more successful characters. And the university is still seen as an important factor in the renewal of human hopes.

CHAPTER 10

Finale

I The Department

THE last novel which was to come from the pen of Gerald W. Brace was published in 1968. The novelist at that time was retired from his regular teaching duties at Boston University but was still teaching a course in creative writing there. His eleventh novel, *The Department,* centered on the life of Robert Sanderling at the point of his retirement, after teaching practically a lifetime at the large city university. Brace was again treating fictionally materials which were quite contemporaneous, though the novel is in the form of a memoir. *The Department* offers further proof of Brace's sustained creative powers. This late novel is among his finest achievements.

Brace had taught at Boston University for the last twenty-nine years of his academic career. It is natural to assume that he was drawing on a good number of his colleagues at least as partial portraits for the fairly large number of professorial characters in this novel. Given the kind of close academic in-fighting that the novel describes, one can readily assume, also, that Brace's own colleagues must have read his book with a great amount of relish, glee, disgruntlement, or anger, as the case may be, regardless of how thoroughly they may have read his several prefatory remarks about the nature of the transmutation of characteristics from life into the fictional entity. One of the hallmarks of Brace the novelist is his integrity and honesty in pursuing the perceived human nature of his fictional subjects. It must have made, to say the least, for some lively moments in the faculty room at Boston University when the novel appeared. As reported in the student paper, Brace told his creative writing class at Boston University the following:

But I also taught at Harvard, Dartmouth, Williams, Amherst, and Mount Holyoke, . . . so the characters are not drawn after anyone on this

campus and very few relate to anybody in particular. As soon as any
character begins to function in a book, he is different from anyone else
on earth. Sanderling's wife, who is closer than most, is not like anyone
around here. I have been discreet.[1]

The reader is well advised by the author in the various prefaces
about the nature of the fictional experience.

Robert Sanderling is in his last semester of teaching. He knows
the format of the retirement ritual he will face shortly. A formal
luncheon with gifts and speeches. He is already preparing the
remarks he will have to make—the polite joking and all the rest.
He feels "too little confidence, too little courage" is what best
sums up his whole career. He is a sensitive man. Passages of
poetry that he loves can still fill him up if he reads them publicly,
but he would rather retire suddenly and duck the rituals. His
wife Harriet, however, is a fighter, and he feels an obligation for
the money that has always been needed. He wrote a novel back
in his early days; it was a fair success but he had failed to carve a
niche for himself by the ordinary means of a professional book,
although he is "supposed" to be an authority on the eighteenth-
century novel. He hovers between the idea of saying something
serious or uttering the usual "urbane clichés."

Sanderling begins a review of his career which of course
becomes *The Department*—a novel in the form of a memoir.
Simon Partridge has just retired the previous spring. He was a
native New Englander like Sanderling, a man of the old school of
oratorical flamboyance who lived near Robert in a house filled
with Victorian pieces emblematic of his life. Partridge had been
chairman of the department for ten years and had been hooked
on the poetry of William Vaughan Moody. Hardly, Sanderling
reflects, the man who should have led other teachers into the
modern era in American poetry. But Partridge's farewell
appearance had been effective. Sanderling admired the "physical and moral assurance standing before us"; Sanderling still
shares a belief "in the Partridge chain of being."

Another dominant figure is the present chairman, George
Willett, sixty-two, the successful administrator, a name-dropper
who has had some association with Scott Fitzgerald but whose
values in literature tend to follow the latest quotations from the
elitist critical stock-market. Willett can't get along with the
creative writing group on the English staff—Merlin, the poet, or
young Findel, the teaching assistant who likes to write scatologi-

cal verse. Sanderling confides that about twenty-five years ago it
was Willett whom Harriet fell in love with. He doesn't pretend to
know precisely what Willett's part in the affair was, but Willett
"had dealt with many women in his life." Sanderling is "normal in
appearance, inconspicuous, five feet ten and a half, a hundred
and seventy pounds, active enough though not rugged." He
keeps in fair shape mostly by walking. He has eschewed faculty
social life by and large; he doesn't care greatly for the drinking.
But, he admits that what kept Harriet and himself together was
her teaching him how to manage martinis. Harriet has the drinks
ready each evening; "here's how," she'd say, and he would
answer, "Cheers." Harriet is a fully emancipated woman, gifted
in many ways. She was an amateur actress. Her sardonic
comments were the life, and sometimes the defeat, of the party.

"Don't you think I was born to be Goneril? An absolute five-star bitch."
I could play her for all she was worth. But, of course, she didn't really
think of herself as a five-star bitch. Her true vision of herself was as
Candida, the wise and dominant female who assumed that all men were
little boys who leaned on her for comfort and flattery. (p. 53)

Sanderling feels their only child, Joan, now married with five
children of her own, was driven to her revolt at sixteen by
Harriet's insistence on art, music, and dramatics. Harriet
"discovered" the small house in Newton where they moved from
their earlier bungalow. Her sardonic views permeated their
early sexual relationships where she charged Sanderling with
being inadequate. Their sexual life together was hectic, resulting
in many quarrels and ultimately their sleeping apart. Sanderling
takes a tolerant view in retrospect, accepting her mockery and
wondering why she didn't try to do away with him when the
occasion of illness had given her the chance. It was about that
time that she began to see Willett.

The Medricks are the moneyed people in the department,
with a large house in Cambridge. Horace Medrick's degrees are
from Chicago and Oxford. He is urbane and gentlemanly.
Their annual dinner party is a highlight of the year. McLoon is
there to play the don, perhaps the most brilliant of the group and
a heavy drinker. So is Grosbeck, the most steady publisher of the
whole staff, who carries his scholarship with a high degree of
hauteur. McLoon has been drinking before Grosbeck arrives and

uttering remarks about his being a damned German Fascist. He delivers the more insulting remarks directly to Grosbeck when he arrives. Grosbeck does not allow a single word of the insinuations to be lost. Willett tries to break it up, but it ends with Grosbeck calling for witnesses, denouncing McLoon as unfit for his position and stomping out of the party despite the further efforts of the hostess and the chairman.

Sanderling refers to his writing as "notes" which he continues to aggregate. He fills us in on his Vermont heritage. His father had come down to Boston as a bank clerk, had gotten into real estate and become a branch manager in Newton. His mother was church-going, virtuous, but not righteous, although she did weep when she found out her son was reading *Tom Jones* in college. Robert has pleasant memories of the farm life at his uncle's in Vermont.

He wonders why he became a college professor since his people were not scholarly. He assumes the Vermont forebears were men of "great moral and physical strength." Compared with Grosbeck, whose family were editors and philosophers, he feels himself a sort of "academic imposter." At Harvard for his graduate study, Sanderling had never felt he belonged. He made a few friends and was instrumental in helping one of them, a Jewish boy, who was having a particularly difficult time of it.

There were four women besides Harriet in Sanderling's life. Characteristically he is reticent but honest in telling the reader about each of them in his "notes." Nora Martin he had known before he met Harriet, and she was next to Harriet in the seriousness of their relationship. She was a Radcliffe student and he was at Harvard. He used to eye her on the street and in the street car. It was a slow process until he maneuvered her to a meeting. Finally he was invited to her home. Her folks were wealthy, but Nora didn't have any airs. Yet the house was a mystery to him. The sensitive Nora alternately responded to Robert and then discouraged him. "A taint of insanity," Nora finally called it. Her brother had to be put away at twenty-seven. She could not be a wife or mother. Sanderling gives her up at Nora's and her family's insistence. Nora dies shortly after. Robert feels that she may have taken her own life.

Judith Samaris was a student in one of Sanderling's large classes. She came to see him on a perfunctory matter and seemed to want to talk: "You like those novels you talk about, don't you?" She was placid and seemed to probe for something more. She would come back and talk. She talked later about guilt and punishment in Smollett and Fielding. She confided that she had a six-year-old daughter and was unmarried. Sanderling was sympathetic and taken by her serious nature. Eventually he realized that what the girl wanted him to know was that she had been prostituting herself for ten years. Sanderling was drawn to her youthful body. "The fact is I loved her." Judith seriously sought wisdom: how to live, how to bring up her daughter. They ended their talks where they began, with *Fanny Hill* and *Tom Jones.*

Harriet is not oblivious to the possibilities of romance for her "Sandy." She goads him about giving "A's" to a beautiful Spanish countess. There is another student, Margery, who drifts into Sanderling's life, although she probably planned things that way. She is a very young freshman from a remote part of Maine and needs a friend at the big university. She is a good student, who slowly grows up in the new environment. It is Margery who does the pursuing, but she does not interfere with Sanderling's work. They stroll along the esplanade or go to Fenway Park. There is little vanity about her. "She was simply carried along on the wonderful tide of pleasure and adventure with a friend, father and lover all at once in a new world of discovery." Harriet meanwhile is preoccupied with George Willett. The spring of Margery's graduation comes round:

Love filled our minds, and if we had had a place to be secret in we would have gone there and made love; we were hardly aware of anything else. (p. 192)

Sanderling meets her parents at graduation ceremony. Margery says to him over and over: "I'll never be alive again."

At the same time Harriet is trying to turn their daughter, Joan, a solidly built large girl, away from her natural inclinations. She fails, although this has been probably what she most wanted to succeed at. But Joan turns out all right—she majors in animal husbandry and fulfills herself as a mother with four sons and a daughter, living in a rural area of New York with a "complex of barns, sheds, pens, corrals, garden plots and land running on indefinitely into fields and woods."

Mark Jaeger is the department's Victorian expert. His Teutonic pride is frequently displayed and Sanderling is the target of the attacks since he took over the Victorian novel course which Sanderling used to teach. Jaeger is a hawk for research, belaboring his fellow teachers for their lack of comprehensiveness. Yet for all his insistence he himself is not productive. His wife is also a German scholar and there are reports of their failure to get along together. Jaeger's lifelong project of special interest is an elaborate study of Dickens's unfinished novel *The Mystery of Edwin Drood*. His students write endless papers on the subject. Jaeger tends toward psychoanalytic criticism— unconscious symbolism, computerized tabulations. He winds up trying to construct an ending for the uncompleted Dickens novel as the master himself must have conceived it. Student complaints mount concerning his ineffectual instruction; Sanderling notices his distractedness and tries to speak to him, but he commits suicide shortly afterwards. Then his colleagues "agreed to admire Jaeger more than we had in his lifetime."

All along Sanderling's best friend is John Piper, who is the American Literature man of the department. He has never taken his doctorate and in time is subjected to criticism from the younger men. His conscientiousness has always been apparent. His wife is a "perfect ineffectual and ignorant woman." The drudgery assignments have fallen his way eventually, and "honest John" has gone on with it but finally simply quits his position within a few years of his retirement. "His indoor face had simply crumpled into age and sadness." Piper fails not so much for inadequate scholarship, but because he is "full of a miserable sense of his own inadequacy in his profession." Together with Partridge and Sanderling himself, Piper has been one of the old New Englanders in the department, a leftover from the genteel tradition. Sanderling feels that he cannot imagine life without some of their common ideals.

As his reflections near an end, Sanderling thinks he might risk in his farewell speech an idea or two, although he is aware that expressing ideas publicly is difficult for him. Is, for example, the academic freedom spoken of so much actually an illusion? Yes, he concludes that it is, but ultimately he is grateful for it.

Sanderling would do it all over again pretty much as he had, despite the Grosbecks who reduce literature to data to be correlated and despite the esoteric nature of the younger psychological critics. He would go along with the humanistic stress, but he knows that "teaching like art, like truth itself is a resolution of many forces and claims."

As he came to the close of his career as a novelist, it was clear Brace had saved the good wine until the last. There is a large tolerance and forbearance toward his fellow human beings in *The Department*. Sanderling may be seen as a person with little self-confidence, a lack due to the particular circumstances of his life. He lacked a cultural background that would have suited him better in the university life. Yet even Harriet admits in her dying hour that "Sandy" has done all right in his career despite her undercutting of practically anything he said or did. Robert Sanderling's life shows a remarkable depth, a great capacity for compassionate understanding of all the persons that enter his life. It may fairly be argued that the imagination, the object in the final analysis of the literary man's study of the kind which Sanderling pursued honestly and faithfully in his long career, was at the heart of the man's moral being and development. Sanderling is particularly self-conscious about his failure to keep up with the newer culture and its modes of literary scholarship; he even feels that he cannot any longer be a guide for the young student. Yet his moral imagination aids him in his own quandary. He tells himself that if he had any opportunity to teach, speak, or write he will go on "representing the faith he has grown up in." The faith that is spoken of is of course not so much a particular denominational religious faith but a way of life grounded in the Christian virtues of his forebears. His father had not troubled himself over a "commitment" to a religious code; he had doubts about religion. Yet his traditional Christian faith sustained him when it came to the moment of his death. His son embodies many of those same virtues, and they have been nurtured in the rich soil of humanistic studies. A good part of Sanderling's strength seems to derive from his awareness and honest pride in his Vermont heritage. Perhaps his habit of helping others is in good part traceable to the rustic virtue of lending a hand when it is needed. This moral spirit in Sanderling is strong enough to carry him through a marriage which seems to have little chance of surviving without his faithfulness to his own humanistic perceptions.

Of course, there are moments when Sanderling feels that the academic life is a "great ferris wheel," that is, a cyclical pattern of existence which he and others merely depend upon for safe conduct between "boyhood and death." But, when moral strength is in demand, Sanderling musters it in sufficient amounts. He is not a professor who is a joiner or even a signer of petitions, but is a man who would stand by a fellow human and do what he could. It is understandable that Sanderling's moral ideas bring him into conflict with his students. Sanderling's student Stanley Weintraub argues for the moral irrelevance of Rashkolnikoff's murder. It wasn't his business to take sides. If Sanderling argues that the rightness of an act is a relevant thing, his modern student retreats. Stanley is "polite enough, he doesn't strongly argue—he may shrug, not in arrogance but as a way of implying that the question is dead. Scientists deal with what is. Artists deal with what is. No one else in his world really counts" (p. 153).

Karsch was a more militant type, a student with some creative writing talent. The story of Brer Rabbit and the Tar Baby as a close focus for the essentials of the fictional form has become a standard favored item in Sanderling's repertoire, until Karsch leads a revolt against what he sees as Sanderling's critical formalism. Karsch turns in endless quantities of manuscript which Sanderling finds hardly comprehensible. Yet he continues to give the cynical Karsch fair treatment, even though he abandons the Brer Rabbit bit in his class presentations.

Another of his former students is Levinson, who is now teaching art in Boston. Sanderling seeks him out to see if he can find out something about how other teachers are conducting their classes. Levinson is a disciple of Significant form. He speaks of EMOTIONAL AWARENESS, the Language of Form and Vocabulary. But he shies away and becomes evasive when Sanderling asks "how about Symbolic Form?" Sanderling thought it would be fruitful perhaps to bring Levinson to his class, even though Karsch would be there. It is a measure of Sanderling's fairness that in the end he felt Karsch had carried the day against the formal aesthetics of Levinson: "I tell myself that I don't really agree with him, but I see what he means."

Sanderling's attitudes here may seem like narrow temporizing. Doesn't the reader after all want to know what Sanderling's own stance is? After all those years in the classroom, doesn't he have any real convictions of his own that he would be willing to defend down the line? The situation has a relevance to the whole action of the novel. Properly understood it is at the heart of the conception of *The Department*. Brace is using Sanderling as an ironic central figure in his story in order to get at the heart of modern life itself. In most of Brace's novels there is a strong implication that if there is any force for a better life it is more likely to be found at the university than elsewhere. The university milieu affords the novelist a wide perspective on many social questions and *The Department* contains one of Brace's most comprehensive views on the human condition. If Sanderling may appear supercautious or even subservient in his interactions with life at the university, it is not because he lacks principles. It is because he recognizes the very great complexity and mystery of the human heart. Sanderling does have clear principles and priorities. These show up throughout the novel in all of his dealings with other people. It is human life that he cares about; it is people that count with him. Sanderling never really vacillates on that score and the same thing should be said for his creator.

The most obvious riches of *The Department* lie in the portraitures of professors. The various figures that come alive in these pages, in the sense of their familiarity to us who associate them with some one or other teacher we have known, are demonstrations enough of Brace's ability to conceive universally human characters. These professors are not simply described in their idiosyncracies (although Brace's novel is rich in its language and in its allusiveness). They come alive as characters in the hands of a man who knows academic infighting at firsthand. Another example of Brace's masterful handling of comic-ironic scene is the two-hour Ph.D. examination of Joseph Mallick by Chairman Willett, Grosbeck, Jaeger, Sanderling, and others. "The game," Brace says, "is a bit like poker; no one betrays himself." But in actuality they all do. Jaeger tries to turn the examination into a platform from which he can sneer at the scholarship of the other professors and promote his own rather twisted ideas. Grosbeck, the bibliographical scholar, leaps into the fray forgetting the student whose only course of wisdom is to hope that he will not be punished too much for his silence or be drawn too much into the cross-fire. Willett has nothing much to offer in this situation except to blow the whistle and try to settle things down. Sanderling acts kindly towards the Ph.D. candidate; he perceives the nervousness and tries to shift the questioning to some common grounds to turn the exam experience into something worthwhile. Mallick passes, but quite possibly only because of the tactfulness that Robert Sanderling brought to the whole situation.

Charles Brady's review of *The Department* brings out with fine discrimination some of the outstanding qualities of this novel.

In *The Department* that surviving Trollopian among our novelists, Gerald Warner Brace, has written an American equivalent of C. P. Snow's *The Masters*. It is a sweet piece of work. Just how sweet may be gauged by measuring it against Cozzen's pretentious *Morning Noon and Night,* which has a similar theme and almost identical structure. The difference lies not only in Brace's greater skill but in his warmer humanity. His personality keeps his observations on life mellow without imparing their satiric tautness. . . . What makes Brace's novel the great success it is, is its wise and witty and basically good-humored anatomy of every English Department that ever was. . . . Both Proust and Wharton used an aquarium image for society. Brace's Academe is rather a comic taxidermist's shop for the old rats in the academic rat-race, with the young rats grouped next door in up-to-date Madame Toussaud postures. . . . Good as it is, the comedy of intellectuals' nuanced inner lives, expressed with a nice economy of effect, is by no means all. Brace is an ethical novelist contemplating the anomaly of college ministers without portfolio. He believes in the imperative knowledge, regrets the disappearance of a sense of beauty and points out that the consequences of vanity are what they have always been.[3]

Sanderling is puzzled by a recurring dream. It is related to the figure of his Aunt Martha as she stood in the doorway of a white clapboard house, just as he remembered her on his visit to Vermont when he was ten. She lived alone in the two storied house in the small town. Of course the passage of time has changed the actual scene, but in Sanderling's mind and dreams the house seemed waiting for his return. It has come to stand for "the serene good place, the pure house, the pure life, the sweet immaculate woman waiting to take me in. This is what I have lived for and yearned for all these years—this actually is what mankind lives for and yearns for" (p. 262). Sanderling sometimes wakes in tears and with a sense of the unreasonableness and the vanity of his dreams. Yet the dream itself is "unquenchable" and, he realizes, that life itself is like dreams "mysteriously rich and strange." Brace's *The Department* is a novel that ultimately gives an affirmation of life.

CHAPTER 11

Brace on the Art of the Novel

The transcendental visions of God and infinite goodness are all diminished, and the question we ask, as Frost puts it in a poem called "The Oven Bird," is what to make of a diminished thing.

G. W. Brace, *The Stuff of Fiction*

GERALD Brace taught English and American literature and creative writing in a half dozen New England colleges or universities ranging over a period of about forty years. His writing primarily was devoted to the craft of fiction; wisely, no doubt, he did not pursue, in writing at least, the formal practice of literary criticism. When he occasionally published an article it was usually in the nature of an overview of the novel, or a text that was printed from a talk to a group of writers or to a university audience.

I *"The Great New England Novel"*

Professor-novelist Brace addressed a conference in 1954 on the subject "The Great New England Novel."[1] He made clear that he considered New England as a microcosm, as one might infer from a reading of his own novels. He addressed himself to the diversity of landscape, weather and thinking that makes up the attractiveness of the region. He went on to explore what the borrowed term, "The Great American Novel," meant for him. He saw in *The Scarlet Letter* a great piece of writing but of an "unreal quality," unrelated almost as the Greek Tragedies are unrelated to our experiences. In *Moby Dick* there was the question of form; it was more epic than novel. Brace felt that Mark Twain was consciously attempting something like The Great American Novel in *The Gilded Age* wherein he collaborated with Charles Dudley Warner. It was a noteworthy experiment in spite of its failure and from that point in American literature there seemed to be a desire on the part of Americans to write "the great one." In more modern times Brace lists the work of Dreiser, Lewis, Dos Passos, Faulkner, and Steinbeck, implying that there have been great American novels by each of these writers. "Perhaps the difference is that we no longer expect only one, but many great novels to come out of America."

What of New England in the modern era? Brace suggests that it might appear as if it had come into the Indian summer of its literary existence. Characteristically he faces the issue squarely. He finds the "ghost of Puritanism" to be misapprehended, especially the idea that repression dominates New England's life. "That notion is generally accepted, and I find that it is a very silly one." Writers have allowed themselves to believe that the removal of repression and restraint is the equivalent of the good life.

Writers should be wary, too, of their sense of nostalgia, or their placing too much emphasis on the idea of the changes being undergone. Marquand's George Apley may be revered by many beyond his earlier significance. By comparison Brace felt that England in its recent coronation ceremonies had "gotten themselves into an almost tragic predicament of living on pride because of their magnificent past, and yet, because they are British, they must not show that pride."

In concluding his remarks Brace did not denigrate the notion of a Great New England Novel. Rather he thought it wasn't a bad idea to have around because like the idea of a Texan epic, or any other, it does stimulate the writer to some extent towards a greater achievement.

II   *"The Age of the Novel"*

Since 1950, two University Lecturers have been nominated each year by the Board of the Graduate School of Boston University from the suggestions of the faculty and of the graduate students. In 1956 Professor Brace was selected by Boston University's President Marsh to give one of these University Lectures for that year. His lecture entitled "The Age of the Novel" incorporated many substantial views on the nature of the novel in English.

In his nonfictional writing Brace was every bit as forceful and as careful a stylist of sentences and paragraphs and themes as he was in the writing of his novels. He began by heralding the preeminence of the novel since the seventeenth century. "Take away the pageant of English fiction and I believe a large part of English civilization, not to say the British Empire itself, would go with it." Inevitably the key question in the lecture was the great changes the novel was undergoing in the modern era. Brace's prime question was: "Are these changes in the form and function of modern fiction chiefly external and superficial or do they intimate some deeper alteration in the nature of man?" Brace was not one to duck the difficult questions.

In seeking an answer Brace recited some of the great characters and great scenes created by the outstanding English and American novelists, stressing how their differing styles grew out of differing "powerful social and personal needs." The new middle classes needed a school, and novelists like Defoe helped more than any other source to fill this need for knowledge. Fiction continued to fulfill this purpose even into our own twentieth century. Dreiser, Arnold Bennett, and Sinclair Lewis, Brace sees as writers who, in their reportial fashion, have continued a prose style that was mainly fashioned by Defoe.

As for the structure of the novel in the eighteenth and nineteenth centuries, it had a strong "folk" quality, "if by folk one may designate all sorts of ordinary and extraordinary people." The novels were written by unliterary amateurs, by young girls, by careless craftsmen (including Scott and the early Dickens), by the pious, the sensitive and the sentimental. There was little in the way of principles, criticism, tradition and "not even very much respectability." Brace recognizes Fielding as the only notable exception before Henry James of an important novelist who seems "to have paid any attention to his art." But the vitality of the others sustained them as well—the vitality and the vigor of youth.

The period in Victorian fiction between *Pickwick* and *Diana of the Crossways* is singled out as the most remarkably productive of all. Brace looks to "the agreements" or "belief and desires" which nourished this amazing achievement of the Victorians. From *Pilgrim's Progress* to George Elliot's *Daniel Deronda* novels were primary vehicles for asserting the puritan faith. And those same writers conceived in their fiction a kind of earthly paradise—the inherited English house and abundant means.

Brace argued that in the age of the novel there was more agreement on the idea of society than today; there was a common "aspiration for English gentility." The great writers, from Richardson, Burney, and Austen to Dickens, Thackeray, Meredith, and even Henry James, all desired rank and privilege, money and position in society. But snobbishness is not the whole picture by any means. It must be thoroughly understood that there was always the vision inherited from the Renaissance of the gentlemanly ideal as seen in such figures as Sir Charles Grandison, Rob Roy, Mr. Darcy, and Trollope's Plantagenet Palliser. It is argued that Dickens, too, is actually the "warmest advocate of the social ideals of his world." Dickens stops short of ever proposing any curb on capitalistic power or any "balance between the rich and poor." The Victorian novelists were on safe ground when they depicted an individual's falling below the accepted social or sexual norm of behavior. This, the world knows, they themselves did on innumerable occasions, up to the time of Thomas Hardy.

When the age of the novel grew towards its close in the early twentieth century, writers were becoming simply less assured of their social and theological bearings:

Among the modern philosophers of art there is a tendency to dismiss subject matter as though it were the indiscriminate clay equally suitable for everything or nothing, but one of the fatal signs of the decline of the novel is that Henry James had less of a subject.[2]

Brace attacks the assumption that because the novel has lost command and direction, that it is evanescing as an art, as well as the implication that since the novel was primarily an instructional vehicle it is no longer needed. The other arts are similarly affected. "Is there somewhere in the center of the conglomeration an indestructible essential art?"

The conclusion of the essay is affirmative. Yes, there is a permanent place for the novel, which is very much like that of drama. The particular advantage of the novel is its "scope and inclusiveness." And it has the "unique capacity to organize life into a single meaningful pattern." And yes, Brace argues consistently, great novels will be achieved once again whenever we "aspire to larger beliefs and commit ourselves to celebration or to ideals or even to worship."

III   *"The Essential Novel"*

In 1965 there followed a somewhat shorter piece, "The Essential Novel," published in the *Texas Quarterly* which pursued the question Brace had raised in "The Age of the Novel." Was there something at the heart of all those great and successful novels which might be called "an indestructible essential art?" It is, of course, a highly significant yet difficult question to grapple with.

Using Joseph Conrad's famous preface to *The Nigger of the Narcissus* as his jumping-off point, Brace accentuates the importance of art in experiencing emotional and spiritual pleasure in the modern world. Conrad stressed how the artist "descends within himself," but when his search is successful he reunites with others. The artist relies on his intuitions; he does not avow any particular system of ideas. In Brace's words: "The essential business of the novel is done irrationally; the only words to define it sound frivolous—words like hunch, impulse, whim, notion. But they are basic to the process."[3]

What disturbs Brace to some extent is the esoteric quality in modern criticism which he correctly affirms is written mostly by professors. He uses examples without identifying the critics— three contemporary articles on Faulkner's *Light in August*. One writer reduces the novel to two kinds of images: the linear discrete image and the curve image; another critic stresses an immobile representation of mobility; a third says Faulkner's novel represents a Buddhist Wheel of the Law which then becomes united with Christian imagery to form a Jungian mandala. Brace is not, in the final analysis, unkind in his attitude toward criticism. He knows college is a necessary modern training ground for writers. He is saying, however, that the universities in rewarding such writing have led young scholar-writers along paths that have not been in the long run so healthy for them, especially when this sort of writing becomes a substitute for the purely creative work of poems or stories.

Brace reiterates his views on the earlier novel and its instructional role and how some novelists in the modern era have continued in it. What he is maintaining is that "unless the novel can achieve a genuinely artistic success, where it has unique opportunities, it will take second place to the journalistic nonfiction which has usurped much of its market." (This prediction, made in 1965, appears to be altogether sound.) Brace maintains that the confessional novel, the chronicle of merely sexual or social rebelliousness, is also passé. That kind of "news" is now very familiar to everyone. Modern prophets of the death of the novel have largely viewed the novel in this light as a form of biography or sociology. The problem is essentially the same for painters; a painter must strive to express his own vision "without reverting to the documentary clichés of his predecessors."

Central to Brace's idea of the novel is its close relationship to drama: "Drama derives from curiosity as to fate—generally, of course, human fate. Will he or won't he, we ask. Struggle, or at least potential motion is proposed—that's the action cited by Aristotle." Joyce is unfavorably compared to Dostoievski on the basis of the tension and movement created between Bloom-Dedalus and between Fyodor-Mitya. Joyce does touch us with the classical pity and fear, but in the central epiphanic scene because we are watching "with the eye of knowledge" more than we are sharing the experience. The question is not of the success of his performance, which is very great, but how far his techniques are fundamentally useful for an evolving and we hope advancing novel.

Returning to Faulkner's *Light in August*, at the end of his essay Brace affirms that symbol in literature "is a device for giving a small event large significance; it is a visible sign of a universal truth. But a symbol in isolation, apart from the human motives and human realities which the work is trying to create, may have little or no intrinsic value."[4] Joe Christmas *does* involve our hearts and our imaginations, but the novel as judged by some modern critics makes one wonder what purpose is served.

Brace's third from last paragraph sums up his views. It is important enough to be quoted in full, since it sheds much light on the writer's own work in the novel:

It will be seen that in my effort to grasp what I have called the essentials of the novel, I have made some commitments, the most obvious of which is that man himself is the beginning and end of artistic effort—more than that, for I must assume that man is of primary importance and that his struggle towards order and wisdom is the major motive of his existence. It is the archetype of all dramatic action, and rests on the hypothesis that the protagonist has some sort of value or significance and that his failure is worth watching and imaginatively

sharing. Human value and purpose—those are the commitments I
make, the minimal ones; without them, art, as I understand it, cannot
exist nor can anything that the word civilization connotes. Disgust with
mankind, or contempt, or cynicism, or anger to the very edge of
madness—any of these is allowable and is often a mighty weapon in the
hands of a militant artist, but nothingness is simply that—the rejection
of the human predicament is too absurd or too hopeless to bother with.
For more than a century the philosophical world has made fun of the
Boston critic Margaret Fuller for her solemn assertion: "I accept the
universe," but I hereby come to her defense. Accepting the universe
may not be quite possible for the finite mind, but it is a brave and noble
commitment. I should be satisfied if I could say I accept mankind.[5]

IV   The Stuff of Fiction

In the preface to his short book *The Stuff of Fiction,* the author
pointedly advises the reader that it is intended to be a practical
guide rather than a text on fictional theory. The book does what
it sets out to do—to direct writers towards greater achievement.
In his introductory remarks he encourages writers of whatever
age or talent to take a page from Frost, "our best poet," and to
seek in writing "the momentary stay against confusion." One
must have the courage to confront the truth and to make of it
what he can. Brace cites his favorite writer Trollope once more
as an example of how the writer must work with his talent. There
is necessarily a greater or lesser amount of vanity in every writer.
He must use this, also, to create his vision.
"Human nature" is the stuff of fiction, its content, but the
writer's presentation, his shaping of it, is what the book is about.
"Good fiction is whatever we are willing to accept; it rests on
hypotheses that are quite tentative and creates symbols that are
not more than metaphors, to be accepted on some occasions and
rejected on others."
Brace's dominant notion of fiction as drama is seen in several
chapters of *The Stuff of Fiction.* In giving advice on planning
one's fiction he stresses the idea that the "major business of the
drama must be created as it actually and immediately occurs in
the mind's eye."
As in his own fiction Brace puts a primary emphasis on
character. Beyond that, dramatic tension of some sort must be
built into the character in his situation. Conflict need not mean,
of course, great events. And there is always the thorny problem

of moral truth, whose ambiguities must be worked out. "What keeps us going is the process itself, the twists and turns, the actions and reactions, the revelation of behavior." But it is necessary for good art that the fiction writer make man in good part responsible for his action.

Brace feels that E. M. Forster's distinction about "round" and "flat" characters is too simple to be effective for the writer. To create stories that contain "believable human truth" is the goal of the writer. Goodness and badness in people may not be avoided or overplayed. "If a writer presumes integrity in himself he must assume it in others and deal with it in designing and building his drama." Henry James's own social biases were "full of dark and even sinister human events."

Whichever point of view the writer chooses for his story, the important thing is to maintain the illusion of life. The reader's pleasure lies in his being able to see and hear and judge the action for himself. The Jamesian manner of combining the impersonal with the personal is what most writers use. It is objective yet it involves us with the fictional person; the reader becomes forgetful of the author's presence and gets interested in the created characters. Brace argues that since the letter is no longer integral to our culture, episolary novels are harder to write. Conrad's Marlow also has some drawbacks, mainly because he has to "fill in and conjecture so much." The modern attempt at recording consciousness, the "interior monologue," is questioned by Brace. "As a controlling point of view for writing fiction, it has a smothering effect." But ultimately any way of gaining the necessary suspenseful curiosity in the reader is a good way—if it actually works.

A recurring thought of Brace is that the inner world is what it chiefly remains for the modern writer. He feels that writers, even our Virginia Woolfs, have not so far articulated inner visions successfully in their fictions: "Words relate mainly to things; they tend to be metaphorical, they have referents, they make comparisons with visible objects. To put it more simply they make sense. Yet words can do miracles; they can aspire to the condition of music, as Pater said, wherein states of mind and feeling seem to exist apart from the landmarks of reasonable experience."[6]

Dialogue in fiction is one of the strongest means the writer has to convey the illusion of reality. To have a character speak in his own voice is to come to believe in him. James is a failure ultimately in this respect because he worked towards a pure dramatic form for his stories and yet he was not a "natural recorder of voices and speech." Brace grants that Trollope is often awkward about getting his novels underway; his beginning expositions are too businesslike. But Trollope also knew how to work the large dramatized scene such as the confrontation of Mr. Crawley and Mrs. Proudie in *The Last Chronicle of Barset.* Writers must especially guard against turning dialogue into a lecture sponsoring their own views.

In concluding his book on the writing of fiction, the author gives his views on style. The accent is not so much on the man himself as upon what he can do with words. Words are also the 'stuff of fiction.' Origins and connotations of words and their symbolic thrusts are very important. Language is our great heritage. "Language has always been the emblem and measure of humanistic values." Beginning writers are often unwilling to work out the basic structure of their sentences—their grammatical and logical constructions. "If, to put it simply, reason has no part in the affair, rational discourse may as well be abandoned." The sentence, like the story, is essentially a drama.

The honesty of the artist, finally, is of large significance. But even truth itself is yet another means the story teller uses to gain his own end—the allegiance of the reader.

As a member of Professor Brace's classes at Boston University during the post World War II years in several courses on the novel, I was often struck with the fervor and downright honesty of the man in his presentations to the class. He never particularly found public address, even in the classroom, enjoyable in the performance. However, one always came away from his classes first of all with the feeling that he had pondered carefully every judgment he had formulated before the group. Whatever was maintained by the professor had the ring of utter sincerity to it. Brace the professor spoke with such conviction, I felt, because Brace the novelist also had penetrated the book under discussion. He had empathized with the author of the novel and imparted to the class a special quality of sympathetic understanding in our approach to the work at hand.

Gerald Brace led a double life. He was a novelist and a teacher-critic. He never confused the two roles. His heart—one can be quite sure of this—was in his creative writing. But the exigencies of his career as a successful professor of English led him into serious thought on the evolution of the novel as an art form. His reflections as glimpsed from various critical writings considered in this chapter are a rich humanistic commentary on the novel itself.

CHAPTER 12

New England Novelist

> The pastoralist must of necessity be a man of sophistication writing for a
> sophisticated audience, for to yearn for the rustic life one must first
> know the great world from which it offers an escape.
>
> John F. Lynen, *The Pastoral Art of Robert Frost*

EVER since his earliest boyhood when his parents first rented and then bought a summer home on the coast of Maine in the Bluehill area in the lower reaches of Penobscot Bay, Gerald Warner Brace conceived of no lovelier earthly paradise than rural New England. He sailed its coastal waters, he tramped over its mountains, he wrote much of his fiction during his summer vacations from teaching at his summer home on Deer Isle. He wrote eleven novels all of which are set in New England, and with the exceptions of two late novels, *Winter Solstice* and *The Department,* are all also centered in rural areas or island communities. Even the two exceptions noted have thematically important flashback or background scenes that pertain to a phase of the characters' lives—rural New England. It is fair to state that Gerald W. Brace worked into his writing a kind of pastoral dream of the good life, as he conceived it. Since he was also a man writing under the general rubric of modern realism, he also provides accounts in his novels of the ways men and women have come to terms with life in this New England microcosm of a larger world. Brace's work is important in this respect because he sees the traditions of New England life in a very richly humanistic way and from a perspective not at all chauvinistic or local colorist.

It may be said further that like Robert Frost, Brace is a transplanted New Englander. Frost himself, although he certainly had New England ancestry, came to Lawrence when his father died and he was eleven. He found himself a region that would provide him the stimulus for creating a world which so many readers have found wonderful to inhabit vicariously for themselves. Brace has been occasionally faulted for not "seeing New Englandly" enough to suit some readers who may be making the fundamental error of expecting the writer to supply them with a picture of *their* New England, the one which admits of no deviations. Brace was a serious writer whose moral vision is worthy of our consideration because he carefully focused over a period of thirty-two years on the changing quality of New England's ways.

Here is how Brace himself summed up the general kind and quality of his writings shortly before he died: "For the most part my novels have not been chronicles of failure, though failure is often lurking like an encroaching shadow. I suppose they belong to the happy-sad genre we call tragi-comedy in which the ironies of disaster represent both an ordeal and a challenge to the spirit."[1] There is a fair amount of accurate self criticism in this statement, just as there is in the following assessment of self: "It seems to me now as I look back that I was immoderately nostalgic and romantic. I saw the world as rich with natural beauty and the possibility of human fulfillment. I saw my people as quietly and faithfully competent and even heroic in their understanding and long sustained struggle to make the best of their destinies. They were for the most part the old-fashioned ones and lived in the same world as their father and grandfathers had lived in. Old farms and their ways, old houses, old ships, old habits and manners and customs—these are the motives of a good many of the novels; but never I hope presented with backward views. I was trying to be candid about the world I had known and lived in and still lived in at the time I was writing. But inevitably my mind grew more and more valedictory."[2]

In *The Islands* (as usually in any fictional structure) there is a basic tension between Edgar Thurlow's love of native land and craftsmanship with boats and his desire to achieve through the more acceptable channels of a university career lending to a professional life. While the resolution is made in favor of the home place, it is also clear that Edgar finally respects the academy. A similar tension can be found in *Light on a Mountain*. Henry Gaunt's opposition to his father's old ways is projected in such a way as to reveal Brace's continuing respect of the Vermont life while at the same time we are witnessing the passage of an era and are recognizing the birth of newer ways of

living. Later on in *The Spire* in the figure of the grown-up Henry
Gaunt we are witnessing a fulfillment. Having chosen a scholarly
career, Henry demonstrates a good balance in his personality as
the new dean at Wyndham College. His stable behavior is seen in
both his social and his intellectual achievements. He is a good
illustration of Brace's ideal in living, i.e., an emphasis upon
classical restraint. When Henry makes a final withdrawal from
Wyndham's deanship after only one year, a firm point is made
about there being no resentment on the Vermonter's part: "I
could normally be very happy here and so could most people. It's
as good a place as there is on earth." In short *The Spire* has
supplied us with a vision of the good life. Brace is the novelist of
the ordinary life, the ordinary man. Wyndham's spire and the
college community itself represent a tradition that Brace himself
has participated in to the fullest and is one which he thinks is of
most importance for the community.

Town and country in opposition with each other and country
getting the better of the bargain is standard fare in pastoral
poems. The singers in famous pastorals are, of course, sophisticated voices giving us an ideal view of rural existence. But they
also try to persuade us to points of view and values that really
imply a truly sophisticated knowledge of men. Brace's books
although they have a strong bias for the country life (the basic
pastoral reflex) often, however, accentuate the role of the
university or knowledge in the lives of all. These opposite worlds
in *The Spire* and in *The Department* are kept in good balance.

The Garretson Chronicle, the book which brought Brace
nearest to the kind of popular reception that all writers naturally
desire, probably expresses best of all his writings the tension
between the traditional New England past and its present. The
difference perhaps between Brace's treatment of Ralph Garretson growing up in the Lost Generation times and the treatment
of similar heroes by more famous American writers of the period
lies in Brace's desire to give the past an importance, to affirm its
value. Ralph realizes acutely the shortcomings of his grandfather
and his father, both of whom lived too much in their shadowy
conceptions and dreams of Compton. Ralph Garretson does not
merely survive in an era of "lostness," he actually manages to
conduct himself with a fair degree of courage and dignity. He is
able to achieve this equilibrium, it becomes clear, because he
learns to sift what was good from what was not so desirable in the

lives of his forebears, all of whom he is able to accept as people. Ralph adopts the rural virtues, generosity, contentment, labor and craftsmanship as modeled in the lives of the Kingsleys. These qualities are essentially in opposition to the too formally perceived notions of class virtue that have been passed along through family snobbery and exclusive prep school regimens. Ralph learns to temper the present with the past just as Seth Kingsley has sought successfully to restore the furniture and wood work of the old Compton houses by patient craftsmanship.

In novels such as *A Summer's Tale* and *The World of Carrick's Cove* it becomes clear that Brace is accentuating the virtues of fidelity, prudence, and love. In the Bracian fantasy situated on August Island, Anthony Wyatt and June Marquis strive to find a life of honesty amidst an outer world of war and tumult. In going heavily into the historical background of the Maine offshore island and by tracing the lineage of his characters to famous people, the author seemed to be illustrating what was possible for man in the modern world. Brace was sounding the possibilities of "what to do with a diminished thing."

In *The World of Carrick's Cove* the novelist wrote a straight-forward reminiscence told by old Ben Carrick about the old ways of life in the small coastal communities. This novel never succumbs to nostalgia but makes its meaning clearly: there were and still are people who live in a spirit of happiness and mutual affection. They do not doubt the worthwhileness of their efforts to reach beauty in their lives. Brace likes to call them "cultural aristocrats." They have worked hard to attain the comfort and security they share with their families. Brace's continuing notion was that this life could be found in the more remote communities of New England or, at least, they provided an opportunity for this kind of life to flourish.

The World of Carrick's Cove is the only work of the novelist which used an other than contemporary setting. The late nineteenth-century pioneering way of life of Ben Carrick gave Brace the opportunity to articulate fully a set of values which he saw in that time and that place of the New England past. It is not an idyllic story because the author grounds the fiction in the felt experience of the islanders. We view their interdependence as well as their independence, their pride of craft as well as their orneriness, their failures as well as their successes. It is a careful revealing of a vision of beauty in American life. Brace was

sharing his version of the past for those readers who were
sensitive enough to see it with him.

Brace's readers, I believe, agree with the author himself that
his mind "grew more and more valedictory." *The World of
Carrick's Cove* although not a mere praise of times past,
nevertheless does not address itself to man's present situation
according to the common notion of what a novel is supposed to
do. And when Brace wrote *Bell's Landing, Winter Solstice,* and
The Wind's Will, he very clearly sketched a sad existence in
suburban postwar New England. These novels show in varying
degree the harshness of life as lived in our cities.

Will Redfern, the hero of *Bell's Landing,* has the memory of
some youthful summers lived by the seashore with his aunts. In
his struggle with sexual desire and with choosing a career he
finally makes some clear headed decisions about love and
friendship—not without spiritual cost. Will's brother casts his lot
with a group of avantgarde writers whose dissolute lives convey
a clear notion of their ultimate worth. Will Redfern is sustained
through his sense of loyalty to other persons: his elderly aunts,
Pop Sardis (his philosophical mentor), and to the Athanakis
family, and to his mother and brother as well. This fundamental
trait of fidelity to persons is one of the most positive and
pervasive of human values to be found in the fiction of G. W.
Brace.

The city is seen for the first time in a Brace novel in full
perspective in *Winter Solstice.* Its suburban life as caught
through the representative lower-middle-class Eustace family is
relentlessly grim save for the sardonic humor of the old father, a
transplanted Vermonter and for the tenacious courage of Mary
Kyle Eustace, his daughter. Mary Kyle's sacrifice of her secret,
sustained passion for the already married John Rossiter, on the
grounds of the essential immorality of a mere liaison with him
shows the novelist's attitude toward licentious behavior. Yet
Winter Solstice succeeds on its own terms; it is another finely
drawn portrait of a modern woman.

In *The Wind's Will* Brace was redoing, but with a more
pronounced dramatic emphasis, a basic situation which had been
developed in his first novel, *The Islands.* David Wayne successfully fights off parental religious fanaticism and family
dishonor and suffers through sexual crises without capitulating to
the forces of town gossip. He maintains his moral equilibrium and

makes a start on his college career. Brace was again undoubtedly running a course counter to what the prevailing behavioristic psychologies would consider normal for such a course of events. Yet the novel is a creditable performance. Brace was exemplifying in this New England life the stuff of human nature, the interplay of mind and will, the formation of a young man.

In his last work of fiction Gerald Brace significantly returned to academe, where he had spent the most of his life, teaching, befriending and above all observing. *The Department* has a rightful claim to a place among his very best fiction. Through the memoirs of Robert Sanderling comes the vision of life that is worth the living, even though he suffers trials of many sorts. What makes Sanderling's existence worthwhile is his acceptance of his limitations, and his willingness to learn from others and from the past. The comic vision of Robert Sanderling comes close to being the comic vision of Gerald Brace. If Sanderling is wrong in anything it is in the assessment of his own worth. He feels himself a "cultural fossil"; of course he is not. He is an example of what is good and important in human endeavor.

In his career as teacher-novelist Gerald Brace lived through a historical period of varied artistic experiment and through many fluctuations of climate in American literary critical thought. While he was an undergraduate early psychological criticism was just beginning to make its way in America; the work of Richards and the Freudian biographies of V. W. Brooks and J. W. Krutch were then being published. While Brace was a graduate student at Harvard in the 1920s the New Humanism of Irving Babbitt was assuming a dominant force in literary interpretation. Brace's Ph.D. thesis reflects his awareness, at least, of the values expressed by the New Humanists. As he began his teaching career in the troubled thirties in Dartmouth and other New England colleges, Marxist criticism was in the ascendance. Then there was the beginnings of aesthetic and formalist criticism which became widely known and taught as a mode of literary interpretation into the forties and after, when Brace was teaching at Boston University and writing many of his novels.

How does one begin to estimate such major influences on the writing of Gerald Brace? In such a varied intellectual and artistic climate, can one properly assess the cross currents that flowed into a man's work? When one realizes what a wealth of reading and study of English and American fiction writers were his, the task becomes all the more improbable. But an approach to the spirit of Brace's work that does seem meaningful is through analogy to one of his early teachers, Robert Frost.

I   *Brace and Robert Frost*

It is generally agreed that, as person as well as artist, Frost represents a way of life that was in a studied manner lived contrary to the general direction that other writers were thought to be taking. He, himself, was a west running brook or a bent birch. Certainly there were other American writers, many of them of the time, who shared similar intellectual inheritances with Frost and carried out humanistic ideals in their thinking and writing. But underlying Frost's appeal was his intensely felt human experiences. Translated into poems, they gripped the reader. They made him think. Hyatt Waggoner says of Frost: "Fundamental in his philosophy is his conception of man's nature. In a period obsessed with the notions that moral ideas are meaningless, reasoning is rationalizing, and all previously held concepts of man's nature have been, somehow, exploded in the laboratory, Frost holds that ideals are real, that ideas are powerful instruments in man's march toward his dream, that man is not merely a body but a spirit as well, that, in other words, intelligence and volition give man a power which is different from the force of a chemical explosion and which no laboratory experiment can prove to be illusory or necessarily doomed to frustration."[3]

In a similar but much more modest fashion, Brace's fiction has been written in a spirit consonant with that of Robert Frost's.

Many writers have recounted how Frost went to Harvard seeking the instruction of William James and how even though he was never fortunate enough to come directly under the famous philosopher, he read James and was influenced by his ideas. The early poems of Frost with their character studies of New England folk can be viewed as a kind of Jamesian laboratory or clinic. Brace, too, adopted New England as his favorite country, even before he, as a sophomore at Amherst College in 1919, studied under Frost. Brace admitted that it took him a few years to really learn how to read Frost's poems. Then he began to associate those authentic voice sounds and characters of the poems with the people he met and remembered on his own explorations of the countryside beyond Amherst. "From this moment Frost penetrated, got under my skin and into my consciousness, became in a way the very voice of the country I was trying to claim." Brace reminds us that another great teacher and scholar at Amherst was encouraging him along similar lines. Professor George Whicher "tried to educate me in the sombre regional naturalism of the times, the helpless clutch of circumstances in which the old society found itself. . . ."[4]

Brace has paid tribute in writing to Frost on other occasions. When writing a short piece on Frost and New Hampshire for a writer's conference, the novelist credits Dean Briggs of Harvard with finally counseling Frost that giving up the study of Latin and Greek might after all be the best thing for him at that time and that Frost had never forgotten this sympathetic understanding at the right moment.

Brace speaks in his autobiography, *Days That Were*, with characteristic modesty and kindness about his friendship with Frost; of how Professor Whicher suggested that Brace, when he lost his position at Dartmouth during the Depression, should look up Frost at Amherst for some advice or help;[5] of how Frost chided him (after reading *Light on a Mountain*) in a good-natured way about not knowing enough about Vermont folk to write a novel about them.[6] Brace's later reflections on Frost (coming after the publication of the last volume of Thompson's biography) represent the great American poet as a difficult person of genius, yet one who could also be most delightful in his friendships. Frost, the self-publicist and troublemaker, is seen by Brace as a man of genius following his own competitive instincts, his own nature.

Rather than what Brace calls the "rooted conservatism" image of Robert Frost given in Lawrence Thompson's work, Brace prefers to stress Frost's constant play of ideas in the poetry: "He was too professionally philosophical, too learned, too cagey, to let himself be caught inside a dogma, though I can see that he leaned toward the conservative Yankee individuality he had been brought up with, an Emersonian self-reliance that took no stock in communal ways of life or even legally enforced equalities."[7]

Brace spoke of Frost as America's best poet. He admired a great many of his poems, both early and late. He is on record as preferring amongst all of them the dramatic monologue "The

Witch of Coos," from the volume *New Hampshire*, which he called "the most brilliant short story in verse in our literature."[8] Brace liked the way Frost could turn small details or objects into "emblems" that radiated larger meaning. It was this quality which, I believe, Brace himself sought often in his own writing. "He [Frost] saw us always as poised and balanced between reason and impulse. . . ."[9] It is this same classical kind of poise and balance that is sought after and achieved, and becomes a characteristic of the Brace novels.

There are of course many obvious divergences in the style and the outlook of the two writers. Frost's poetry is rooted in the soil, New England farm life, while Brace's novels, although they show a great love of rural scene and folkways, do stress thematically very often the need for the university intellectual training and development and its ongoing quest for truth. Brace's life, as his autobiography shows, was a calmer, more stabilized experience as compared with the turbulent hectic and tragedy-prone existence of Frost. Brace was fortunate to have had a family background of moderate wealth; Frost knew economic hardship early and it appeared to have largely conditioned some of the difficult attitudes of his later years.

In religious matters both writers may be termed agnostic in their attitudes towards Christian orthodoxy. Yet Frost, I believe, is properly called a poet who is deeply concerned with man's relationship to God. The much-cited late poem "Directive" can hardly be construed in any other fashion than of a poet's thirst for the Creator. Likewise I feel that Brace's apparent agnosticism with its tough prevailing coat of realism speaks in undertones its conviction that man desperately needs his God, needs to find a new faith in Him, and that man regrettably often loses sight of his ancestor's achievements in faith.

I do not mean to make the comparison between Frost and Brace a kind of blanket "influence." I wish merely to indicate that one of Brace's strongest feelings was a love of New England and its people that readers of Frost know so well from his poems, poems that have indelibly captured that love and that trial of existence. Many of the tones of Frost's poetry are found also in the novels of Brace.

It is fair to say likewise that the novels of Anthony Trollope, which Brace rated so very highly for their achievement as prose fiction of the English language, were a continuing inspiration for him in his own writing and that there are enough stylistic resemblances between the two writers to bear out this contention. Beyond that it is sufficient to say that Gerald W. Brace in a writing career that spanned forty years of the mid-twentieth century in America, wrote eleven novels which are noteworthy for their continuing excellence of craftsmanship, their realistic chronicling of the life of "ordinary" people of New England, and their underlying moral perspective rooted in a classical conception of mankind.

Notes and References

Chapter One

1. Harriet Beecher Stowe, *Old Town Folks* (Cambridge, Mass., 1869), p. 250.
2. Gerald W. Brace, *Days That Were* (New York, 1976). Page references appear in the text.

Chapter Two

1. *The Stuff of Fiction* (New York, 1969), pp. 17–18.
2. Brace, *The Islands* (New York, 1936), pp. 20–21.
3. Ibid., p. 223.
4. "Gerald W. Brace; Teacher-Novelist," *College English* 18 (December 1956): 157–58.
5. "I Traveled a Good Deal in Amherst," *Amherst Alumni News* (Winter 1963): 8.
6. Review of *The Islands, New York Herald Tribune Books,* May 31, 1936, p. 5.
7. "I Traveled," p. 4.
8. *The Wayward Pilgrims* (New York, 1938), p. 11.
9. "I Traveled," p. 7.
10. *The Wayward Pilgrims,* p. 135.
11. August 1938, p. 18.
12. April 27, 1938, p. 10.
13. April 16, 1938, p. 7.
14. *Saturday Review of Literature,* May 28, 1938, p. 19.
15. *Days That Were* pp. 202–204.
16. "I Traveled," p. 7.

Chapter Three

1. *Light on a Mountain* (New York, 1941). Page references in the text.
2. *Cavalcade of the American Novel* (New York, 1952), p. 460.
3. *Days That Were,* p. 184.
4. "I Traveled," p. 7.

Chapter Four

1. *The Garretson Chronicle* (New York, 1964). Page references in the text.
2. *Cavalcade of the American Novel,* p. 458.
3. "The Cult of Experience in American Writing," in *Image and Idea* (Norfolk, Conn., 1949), p. 15ff.
4. Introduction to *The Garretson Chronicle* (New York, 1964) p. xvii.
5. (New York, 1936), p. v.
6. "John Philip Marquand: Martini Age Victorian," in *Fifty Years of the American Novel,* ed. H. Gardiner (New York, 1951), pp. 134, 112.

Chapter Five

1. Letter from George Brockway to Storer Lunt, October 21, 1946. In Gerald W. Brace file at W. W. Norton Co., New York.
2. *Cavalcade of the American Novel,* p. 458.
3. Louise Dickinson Rich, *State O'Maine* (New York, 1964), pp. 23–43.
4. July 1949, pp. 82–83.
5. June 1949, pp. 97–98.
6. June 12, 1949, p. 7.
7. (New York, 1966), pp. 39–40.
8. From an unpublished work by G. W. Brace, read at his home in Belmont, Massachusetts, through the courtesy of Mrs. Brace.
9. Ibid.

Chapter Six

1. *The Spire* (New York, 1952). Page references in the text.
2. Introduction to *The Last Chronicle of Barset* (New York, 1964). Page references in the text.
3. C. P. Snow, *Trollope, His Life and Art* (New York, 1975), pp. 9, 15.
4. Letter from Gerald W. Brace to George Brockway, June 25, 1948.

Chapter Seven

1. Letter from Gerald W. Brace to George Brockway, January 21, 1955.
2. *Bell's Landing* (New York, 1955). Page references in the text.

Chapter Eight

1. *The World of Carrick's Cove* (New York, 1957). Page references in the text.
2. Review of *The World of Carrick's Cove,* in *Saturday Review,* August 31, 1957, p. 15.
3. Letter from Gerald W. Brace to George Brockway, February 26, 1957.
4. Letter from George Brockway to Gerald W. Brace, February 26, 1957.

Chapter Nine

1. *Winter Solstice* (New York, 1960). Page references in the text.
2. *The Wind's Will* (New York, 1964). Page references in the text.
3. R. V. Camill in *Book Week,* September 27, 1964, p. 22.
4. *New York Times,* September 27, 1964, p. 5.

Chapter Ten

1. *Boston University Alumni News,* January 23, 1969, p. 5.
2. *The Department* (New York, 1968). Page references in the text.
3. *Buffalo Evening News,* September 21, 1968, p. B-12.

Chapter Eleven

1. *New Hampshire Alumnus,* March 1954, p. 20.
2. (Boston University Press, 1957), p. 19.
3. *Texas Quarterly,* Spring 1965, p. 28.
4. Ibid., p. 36.
5. Ibid., pp. 36–37.
6. *Stuff of Fiction,* p. 111.

Chapter Twelve

1. From an unpublished work by G. W. Brace, read at his home in Belmont, Massachusetts, through the courtesy of Mrs. Brace, p. 12.
2. Ibid., p. 3.
3. "Humanistic Idealism in Robert Frost," *American Literature,* Vol. 17 (1945): 216–17.
4. Brace, "I Traveled," p. 6.
5. (New York, 1976), p. 208.
6. Brace, "Friends Remembering Frost," pp. 22–23.

7. *Days That Were*, p. 210.
8. "Robert Frost's New Hampshire," p. 19.
9. *Days That Were*, p. 210.

Selected Bibliography

PRIMARY SOURCES

All items arranged chronologically.

1. Novels
The Islands. New York: G. P. Putnam's Sons, 1936.
The Wayward Pilgrims. New York: G. P. Putnam's Sons, 1938.
Light on a Mountain. New York: G. P. Putnam's Sons, 1941.
The Garretson Chronicle. New York: W. W. Norton and Co., 1947.
A Summer's Tale. New York: W. W. Norton and Co., 1949.
The Spire. New York: W. W. Norton and Co., 1952.
Bell's Landing. New York: W. W. Norton and Co., 1955.
The World of Carrick's Cove. New York: W. W. Norton and Co., 1957.
Winter Solstice. New York: W. W. Norton and Co., 1960.
The Wind's Will. New York: W. W. Norton and Co., 1964.
The Department. New York: W. W. Norton and Co., 1968.

2. Short Fiction
"Artisans and Models," *Maclean's,* May 15, 1936, p. 7ff.
"Deep Water Man," in *The Story Survey,* ed. Harold Blodgett. New York: J. B. Lippincott, Co., 1939, pp. 320–34.

3. Nonfiction
Between Wind and Water. New York: W. W. Norton and Co., 1966.
The Stuff of Fiction. New York: W. W. Norton and Co., 1969.
Days That Were. New York: W. W. Norton and Co., 1976.

4. Miscellaneous Prose
Introduction to *The Last Chronicle of Barset.* New York: W. W. Norton and Co., 1964, p. xv.
"The Damn'd Profession," *Writer's Monthly,* June 1936, pp. 180–82.
"The Great New England Novel," *New Hampshire Alumnus,* March 1954, pp. 18–19.
"Robert Frost's New Hampshire," *New Hampshire Profiles,* May 1955.
"The Age of the Novel," Reprint of Lecture Boston University Press, 1957, p. 19.
"I Traveled a Good Deal in Amherst," *Amherst Alumni News,* Winter 1963, pp. 1–8.

"The Essential Novel", *Texas Quarterly* 8 (Spring 1965): 28-38.
"What Is Left for the Winter," *Bun State Librarian* 55 (1965): 3-4, 15.
"Friends Remembering Robert Frost" (transcript of Brace's remarks at Special Program of Phi Beta Kappa at Boston University, October 19, 1976, Boston, Massachusetts, 1977), pp. 21-27.

5. Doctoral Thesis
"A Study of Literature in Its Relation to the Fine Arts in England 1650-1750," 1930, Conant Library, Harvard University.

SECONDARY SOURCES

BRADY, CHARLES A. Review of *The Department, Buffalo Evening News,* September 21, 1968, p. B-12. Brady's review is one of the most penetrating of all readings of Brace. He goes to the core of Brace's humanistic vision in this review. *The Department* is favorably compared with C. P. Snow's *The Masters.* Brady cites Brace for his "good-humored anatomy of every English department that ever was."

COFFIN, ROBERT P. TRISTRAM. Review of *The Islands, New York Herald Tribune* ("Books"), May 31, 1936, p. 5. Coffin gives the reader a good appraisal of Brace's handling of Maine folks, customs, and ideas.

HARRIS, ARTHUR S., JR. "G. W. Brace: Teacher-Novelist," *College English* 18, December 1956: 157-61. Harris analyzes briefly the novels through *Bell's Landing,* where he claims Brace finally "comes to grips with passion." He comments also on prose style, pace, and sense of time in the novels.

HICKS, GRANVILLE. Review of *Winter Solstice, Saturday Review,* August 20, 1960, p. 16. Hicks pauses in his review to cite Brace for the consistently fine craftsmanship in the rest of his novels.

HOLMAN, C. HUGH. Introduction to the paperback *The Garretson Chronicle.* New York: W. W. Norton and Co., 1964, pp. v-xviii. These thirteen pages are unquestionably the most solid critical effort thus far expended on Gerald W. Brace's fiction. They provide the beginning reader of Brace with an excellent overview of his writing through *Winter Solstice.* Holman concentrates on Brace's fine craftsmanship and his comic irony, especially in *The Garretson Chronicle.*

WAGENKNECHT, EDWARD. *Calvacade of the American Novel.* New York: Henry Holt, 1952, pp. 457-460. Contains a nearly three-page survey of Brace's first five novels. Wagenknecht is discriminating and generally sympathetic and insightful toward his departmental colleague at Boston University.

Index

Allen, Walter, 103
Anderson, Sherwood, 65
Arcadia, 88
Art of the Novel, 158–67
Atlantic, The, 42, 85
Austen, Jane, 103, 161

Bellamy, Joe David, 63
Belloc, Hilaire, 23, 44
Bennett, Arnold, 160
Benet, William Rose, 43
Borges, Jorge Luis, 34
"Boy's Will, A", 144
Brace, Barbara (daughter), 19, 23
Brace, Charles Loring (grandfather), 18, 19
Brace, Charles Loring II (father), 18, 19
Brace, Charles (brother), 18
Brace, Charles Loring (son), 23
Brace, Dorothy (sister), 18
Brace, Eleanor (sister), 18, 23
Brace, John Pierce (great grandfather), 17
Brace, Gerald Warner; ancestry, birth, childhood, 17–19; attitude toward New England, 168–70, 172; career as a teacher-novelist, 166, 173–75; college career, 20–23; early education, 20; early literary influences, 17, 18–24, 25; the lasting influence of Frost, 174–77; marriage, 23; young manhood, 20–21

WORKS: FICTION
Bell's Landing, 31, 106–117, 172
Department, The, 23, 91, 103, 148–57, 168, 170, 173
Garretson Chronicle, The, 18, 20, 26, 58–77, 78, 91, 106, 126, 170

Islands, The, 26–30, 31–33, 34, 35, 36, 52, 56, 70, 72, 76, 78, 169, 172
Light on a Mountain, The, 45, 46–57, 70, 76, 78, 91, 169, 175
Spire, The, 56, 91–105, 170
Summer's Tale, A, 25, 69, 78–90, 171
Wayward Pilgrims, The, 34–45, 46, 52, 55, 70, 76, 78
Wind's Will, The, 138–47, 172
Winter's Solstice, 103, 126–38, 144–48, 168, 172
World of Carrick's Cove, The, 118–25, 126, 171–72

WORKS: NON-FICTION
Between Wind and Water, 86
Days That Were, 17, 19, 22, 23, 44, 55, 102, 104
Stuff of Fiction, The, 25, 164

Brace, Gerald Warner Jr. (son), 23
Brady, Dr. Charles A., 75, 157
Briggs, Russel Lebaron, 23
Brockway, George P., 79, 102, 106, 124
Browne, Thomas, 135
Bryce, James, 18
Burney, William A., 161
Bushnell, Horace, 18

Cather, Willa, 25, 48, 73–74, 76
Chaucer, Geoffrey, 38, 101–102
Coffin, Robert P. Tristram, 32
Conrad, Joseph, 68, 131, 162
Cooper, James Fenimore, 17
Country of the Pointed Firs, The, 30
Cranford, 31

Daisy Miller, 62
Daniel Deronda, 160

185